Individualized Religion

Bloomsbury Advances in Religious Studies

Series Editors: Bettina E. Schmidt, Steven Sutcliffe and Will Sweetman

Founding Editors: James Cox and Peggy Morgan

Bloomsbury Advances in Religious Studies publishes cutting-edge research in the Study of Religion/s. The series draws on anthropological, ethnographical, historical, sociological and textual methods amongst others. Topics are diverse, but each publication integrates theoretical analysis with empirical data. The series aims to refresh the interdisciplinary agenda in new evidence-based studies of 'religion'.

Individualized Religion

Practitioners and Their Communities

Claire Wanless

BLOOMSBURY ACADEMIC
LONDON • NEW YORK • OXFORD • NEW DELHI • SYDNEY

BLOOMSBURY ACADEMIC
Bloomsbury Publishing Plc
50 Bedford Square, London, WC1B 3DP, UK
1385 Broadway, New York, NY 10018, USA
29 Earlsfort Terrace, Dublin 2, Ireland

BLOOMSBURY, BLOOMSBURY ACADEMIC and the Diana logo are trademarks
of Bloomsbury Publishing Plc

First published in Great Britain 2021
Paperback edition published 2023

A catalogue record for this book is available from the British Library.

Library of Congress Control Number: 2021930321

ISBN: HB: 978-1-3501-8250-9
PB: 978-1-3502-3412-3
ePDF: 978-1-3501-8251-6
eBook: 978-1-3501-8252-3

Series: Bloomsbury Advances in Religious Studies

Typeset by Deanta Global Publishing Services, Chennai, India
Printed and bound in Great Britain

To find out more about our authors and books visit www.bloomsbury.com and
sign up for our newsletters

For James

Contents

Figures

Acknowledgements

I would first like to thank my husband James Wanless, for his ongoing understanding and support. Next, I thank my PhD supervisors, Paul-François Tremlett and Marion Bowman for their unswerving support, fair and constructive criticisms and wise counsel. I am also grateful to many academics and other individuals for stimulating and useful discussions, many of which have challenged my thinking and helped me to move my ideas on. They are unfortunately too many to mention individually here. Finally, I am grateful to everyone I encountered during the course of my fieldwork in Hebden Bridge and the surrounding area – especially my research participants, but also everyone with whom I spent time, talked and engaged with, and shared activities.

In addition, I am extremely grateful to the Open University for the initial support that enabled this project to get started, and to the Arts and Humanities Research Council / CHASE Doctoral Training Partnership for the funding that supported the research during its final two years.

1

Introduction

Alongside the apparent decline of traditional religious institutions in Britain, there has been increasing recognition of the importance of more personal (and personalized) forms of religious expression. Despite this, individualized religion as a phenomenon in its own right remains under-researched and poorly understood. At the same time, however, individualized religion has received what might be regarded as something of a bad press, both in the academic literature and in wider discourse. Much (though not all) of the writing about individualized religion tends to the view that such forms of religion are structurally self-defeating, or trivial, or both. Because these deficiencies are often cited as contributing to the overall decline of religion in the UK and other Western societies, it would seem imperative to improve our understanding of this milieu. The main purpose of the research on which this book is based was therefore to provide both empirical evidence and theoretical tools to aid the study of individualized religion, and to inform ongoing debates about its place in the wider religious landscape.

It is worth beginning by establishing the sense in which I am using certain key terms. First, following what has become fairly common practice, I do not attempt to define what I mean by the term 'religion', but instead use it as a kind of family-resemblance term to denote activities, ideas and practices that look something like a common-sense understanding of what religion entails. Specifically, I am using it to relate both to such activity when undertaken in a group or organizational setting and when undertaken individually. It is worth noting that this is a more inclusive usage of the word than would be common among my research participants since many of them would use 'religion' to refer to religion specifically as it is understood and practised within (usually but not always Christian) institutions. I refer to this latter, narrower concept of religion as 'institutionalized religion', or Christianity. I adopt this wider terminology because unlike my participants (who for the most part want to make their own practice as distinct as possible from an institutional milieu that they tend to mistrust), I want to avoid prejudging the existence of any distinction between institutionalized religion and individualized religion beyond the structural differences arising from their respective levels of individualization.

In this book, I use 'individualized religion' to pick out the kind of religious activity in which the individual and their personal experience are the primary unit of consideration and site of decision making. Many authors have identified an increase in the predominance of this kind of practice, but among the most influential has been Paul Heelas, whose terminology evolved from 'self-spirituality' to 'inner-life spirituality' (Heelas, 1996, 27, 33), and then later with Linda Woodhead to 'subjective-life spirituality' with its additional connotations of a contemporary subjective turn in the ways that religion is practised and organized (Heelas and Woodhead, 2005, 2–7). Grace Davie's concept of 'believing without belonging' also invokes a shift towards greater personal direction by people over the ways in which religion plays out in their lives (Davie, 1994, 107). For Steve Bruce, it is in part the individualization of religious institutions that has led to their ongoing decline in social significance (Bruce, 2003, 61). All these, and the many other formulations of religion as individualized, carry their own contexts and connotations. To chart a way through I have settled on a formulation that allows engagement with each, while allowing for their differences in emphasis. For the purposes of this book, therefore, individualized religion is religion where subjective experience is prioritized, and authority is placed primarily at the level of the individual practitioner. The prioritization of subjective experience speaks to a placing of how things appear to the individual practitioner as above how others tell them things are. The positioning of authority at the level of the individual then affords the practitioner the right to act on their religious impulse in ways they see fit rather than in ways that others tell them are correct or appropriate. While both of these can be seen as important by practitioners, neither of them is a binary. It is possible, therefore, to conceive of a spectrum of individualization, with any particular instance of religious practice being individualized to the extent that it prioritizes subjectivity and places authority at the level of the individual.

One further point to note here is that, when talking about individualized religion, there are two ways in which the term may be used. First, it could be used in a static sense, simply as an indicator of activity that fits the conditions discussed above, to whatever degree. Alternatively, it could be used in a dynamic sense to describe a process whereby pre-existing religious forms or institutions become more individualized than hitherto. Both of these senses are important, and both are used in this book. However, it is important to bear in mind with respect to questions about (for example) how individualization of religion affects its functional viability, that the answer may not be the same in each case, since the assumptions underlying the initial status matter. As we shall see later on, when discussing arguments around secularization theory, this distinction is key.

This book, then, has two primary aims. The first is to elucidate the concept and phenomenon of individualized religion. In doing so, it reports on my ethnographic research on individualized religious practitioners in and around Hebden Bridge (a former textile town in West Yorkshire, northern England), and utilizes data and theory derived from that research. However, the book also engages with the specific question of the social significance, functional viability and transmissibility of individualized religion, with particular respect to its treatment in discussions around secularization. Examining in detail the theory behind the use of notions of individualized religion in these debates not only helps advance those discussions but also sheds new light on individualized religion as a phenomenon in its own right.

Before I set out the overall argument of the book and summarize the chapter structure, I shall therefore begin by briefly setting out my arguments with respect to secularization and secularization theory. Note that my aim here is not to provide a counterargument to the secularization thesis, but to add nuance to the debate by showing how emergent forms of religiosity with radically different logics of organization may have the functional capability to have social significance and to transmit themselves over time.

Is individualization a secularizing phenomenon?

The details and emphases of the various arguments behind the secularization thesis are complex (see Chapter 2), but the view that individualized and non-institutionalized forms of religion are structurally unsuited to social significance and to transmission is a common theme. Among the most rigorously argued cases for this is that put forward by Steve Bruce in his 2011 work *Secularization: In Defence of an Unfashionable Theory* (Bruce, 2011, 112–19). Bruce argues that as religion becomes more individualized, it becomes harder to maintain commitment, since there is no 'external power that the group can mobilize to press the weaker members to do what is right' (Bruce, 2011, 114). Consensus becomes difficult to maintain without recourse to coercion, which means that the movement cannot work together successfully (Bruce, 2011, 114).

The eclecticism of the individualized milieu leads to a lack of cohesion in which elements of religions become removed from their spiritual content, co-opted and trivialized (Bruce, 2011, 116–17). And finally, because there is no commonly accepted set of religious truths, there is no inherent impetus to evangelize (Bruce, 2011, 117–18). Bruce argues that these structural features are inherent to individualized religion precisely because of its individualized status, and that they tend to mitigate both against socially significant practice and against transmission (especially intergenerational transmission) (Bruce, 2011, 19, 117–18).

This argument is proximally framed with respect to moves towards individualization of formerly less individualized religious institutions. This is because it is primarily intended as part of an analysis of how religious institutions and edifices in Britain have lost social significance and the ability to transmit themselves over time. To that extent Bruce's argument is not only sound but compelling, and I agree with him that in this sense individualization is likely a secularizing phenomenon. The reason that it works for such cases is because they concern institutions whose existence is bound up with their respective institutional identities, structures and truths. When such an entity opens up, and allows its members freer rein to develop their own behaviours and ideas, then it does indeed seem plausible that the consequent challenge both to the institution and to the culture and truths that it maintains could be profound, even perhaps existential. Bruce's analysis therefore serves as a very good explanation of how and why religious institutions have lost their social significance and their ability to transmit their ideas and practices over generations in the UK and similar societies. As he rightly argues (e.g. Bruce, 2011, 47–8), such institutions will find it difficult to contain increasing numbers of adherents who see their involvement in more individualized terms without challenge to the organizational structures, and consequently their capability to act as institutions or to self-sustain. However, Bruce makes it clear that he intends this argument to also apply to individualized religion more broadly, including the more static sense of cases of religious activity predicated on individualized structures. Even in such cases, he regards the epistemic individualism that underpins individualized religion as ultimately undermining of its ability to sustain itself over time (Bruce, 2011, 113, 119). I find this usage of the analysis more problematic, because it misses the very real likelihood that social significance and onward transmission of individualized religion outside of and independent to traditional institutions might occur in very different, more individualized, ways and be predicated on different, more subjectivized, social and cultural forms.

The basic underlying incompatibility here is between activity that prioritizes subjectivity and institutions that predicate themselves on claims to objectivity. By 'prioritizing subjectivity', here, I mean activity that affords primacy to subjective points of view. By 'claims to objectivity' I mean acceptance of an internally accepted objective religious viewpoint that is best known to, and promulgated by, key institutional authorities and that is given precedence over subjectively held views. Individualized religion, by my definition, prioritizes subjectivity and takes the individual as a prime location of religious authority. In this milieu, how things seem to individuals is of prime importance, even if others disagree. Traditional religious institutions on the other hand commonly (though not universally) predicate themselves on internally recognized objective religious truths in the form of dogmas, doctrines and accepted practices. They then also tend to contain institutional structures, ideologies and agents that act as holders of religious authority and that can (in theory at least) override an individual's view. All of these would be (and are) undermined by moves towards greater levels of individualization. However, if individualized religion is to be taken seriously as a religious structural form, it must be acknowledged that those involved in it will do things in ways that make sense to them. If an individualized religious milieu were to exist that could have social significance and sustain itself and its ideas and practices over time, this clearly would be done in ways that also prioritize subjectivity and place authority at the level of the individual. Institutions and forms such as those of institutionalized religion would not be able to maintain themselves over time, but this would likely matter neither to practitioners nor to the survival of the milieu. A primary goal of the ethnographic investigation on which this book is based was to investigate whether feasible routes for this to take place might exist, both in theory and in practice.

It is important to recognize, however, that religion does not necessarily sharply divide itself into institutional and individualized forms. By contrast, practitioners may involve themselves in institutions while also maintaining more individualized aspects to their practice, and most religious contexts would be expected to have a rich and complex combination of subjective and objective aspects. Adherents therefore likely negotiate between subjectivity and objectivity in multiple and sometimes inconsistent ways. My ethnographic focus on practitioners that have a strong emphasis on subjectivity is in part a heuristic device intended to shine a light on these complex relationships more widely.

It will be useful here to examine Bruce's specific sub-arguments with respect to commitment, consensus, cohesion and evangelization in more detail, providing suggestions as to what alternative potential routes to social significance and mechanisms of transmission may be available to practitioners operating in an individualized milieu. First, Bruce argues that increasing levels of individualism lead to increasing difficulties for an ideological movement in extracting commitment from adherents (Bruce, 2011, 114). The sense is that if people do not feel that there is some external driver to instil commitment, adherents will be less likely to put the effort in that is required to keep the movement running. While this argument does make sense, it does so for a movement that is coterminous with a specific set of institutional or community structures, to the extent that if they fail the movement itself could also be said to have failed. However, if a movement is structured along individualized lines, then its members' commitment will be to the values and ideas that they perceive as important, and not to specific social or institutional structures. Any commitment that a member will have to groups or their proximal goals will likely take the form of direct commitment to those goals, to the higher purpose of the movement as that member perceives it, and to personal relationships with other group members. Groups and other social structures of various kinds might well be used by such individuals in order to engage and work together, but in themselves would be relatively expendable. If an individual were to cease to find a social structure conducive to the aim to which that individual is committed, or if s/he had personal difficulties with other group members, then that individual might well be likely to move away from that group. Enough people moving away might even mean the end of the group. But crucially, this need not constitute the end of the movement, since those individuals would be free and potentially willing to create new replacement groups built on the lessons of what has gone before. An alternative model of commitment that might therefore exist in an individualized milieu is one in which commitment is not to institutions or specific structures, but to ideologies, goals and personal relationships. Commitment to any kind of structure of engagement is likely to be temporary and contingent on its utility as perceived by its individual members, and to transfer readily to any successor structures. Commitment is not something that is instigated into adherents by officers *in spite* of the adherents' personal proclivities, but instead is something that *arises from* those adherents' personal proclivities. Crucially, in this context, people's ability to work together, and therefore have social significance on a large scale, can transcend both the life and the extent of any particular group structure.

Bruce's arguments about consensus and cohesion (Bruce, 2011, 114–17) are subject to critique on similar grounds. He argues that consensus equates to group discipline (i.e. acquiescence to a movement's claims of objective knowledge), and is broadly something to be engineered through the control of members (through coercion, inspiration or manipulation). In individualized contexts, inability to wield such control successfully arises from the freedom of the individual to decide for themselves what to think and how to behave, and especially their perceived freedom to leave the group at will. Bruce argues that this leads to an inherent weakness in the movement, which is ultimately likely to lead to its failure. He does acknowledge that individualized religion tends to form different kinds of structures, and indeed suggests a pattern of serial and changing memberships (Bruce, 2011, 115). However, because he is identifying socially significant religious movements with functioning institutions, he sees this as a sign of social ineffectiveness (Bruce, 2011, 115–16). But far from being a weakness, this kind of social engagement can in fact be a strength, since it allows for a community as a whole to be more flexible and responsive in its thinking and its activities. Consensus in this context can arise not from acquiescence to a set of objective religious truths, but from a shared ongoing sense of negotiation that uses a range of tools to create a common ground of values, core ideas and relationships. These tools can include (for example) the use of ambiguity and vagueness, acceptance of contradiction, acceptance of contingency, use of shared non-verbal experiences and a focus on shared proximal goals. Arguably this common ground is what more accurately defines the boundaries of the movement – although its own flexible and crowd-sourced nature suggests that these boundaries are likely to be fuzzy, open and diffuse. Social and institutional structures may rise and fall within this common ground, but the potential social strength of the movement as an ongoing cooperative entity likely depends not on the continued existence of those groups but on the life course of the common ground of shared values, ideas and relationships.

Similarly, Bruce's argument about cohesion (Bruce, 2011, 116–17) suggests that in the absence of external authorities, religious elements (such as meditation) can become divorced from their religious underpinnings, and that they are then likely to become trivialized. This constitutes a claim that eclecticism tends to lead to religious dead-ends. However, the levels and multiplicities of engagement that the current research shows are open to individualized religious practitioners indicates that, far from inhabiting dead-ends of trivialism, practitioners are able to use religious elements in numerous novel ways, and in effect create a relatively fertile environment of experimentation and productive discourse and praxis. There is therefore every possibility of significant religious strands emerging and/or sustaining themselves over time. Lack of cohesion is not a weakness of individualized religion with respect to its religious and social significance, but rather a strength.

For religious ideas and practices to be self-sustaining, however, there have to be viable routes of transmission available to them. Bruce argues that in individualized milieus there tends to be little appetite for evangelization due to the emphasis on subjectivity (Bruce, 2011, 117–18). This is certainly a persuasive argument against the feasibility of transmission of cohesive bodies of accepted religious knowledge. However, because internally agreed objective bodies of knowledge are not relevant to individualized practitioners, neither is their transmission. Instead, in an environment that is flexible and open, and in which authority exists at the level of the individual, it makes sense to think of transmission as working in a much more fine-grained way. That is, it makes sense to think of ideas, snippets of knowledge, practices and connections as being the things that are transmitted, together with potential ways of thinking about and working with all these things. Individuals then are free to agree or disagree with one another to whatever degree, while maintaining meaningful religious and social engagement (or not, as the case may be). This is likely to be facilitated by the tools mentioned earlier, namely use of ambiguity and vagueness, acceptance of contradiction, acceptance of contingency, use of shared non-verbal experiences and focus on shared proximal goals, since these can provide nodes of fruitful negotiation.

The argument

The overarching argument of this book is that individualized religious practice has available to it forms of association that can enable it to have both social and religious significance. The population of individualized religious practitioners around Hebden Bridge who were the subject of this research is an example of a context where these forms can be observed in practice. The forms of association that exist among this population are predicated on their understanding of themselves as individualized (and are structurally dependent on that individualized status), but also on a self-replicating ideology of mutuality. This ideology contains the following elements. First, it places the individual practitioner at its heart, framing individuals as self-governing sites of agency, as centres of religious experience, and as able to form deep relationships with one another as well as with a host of non-human entities. It rejects social hierarchies, and places both religious authority and a consequent sense of responsibility at the level of the individual. Equally important, there is also an emphasis on empathy, caring and collaboration, all predicated on notions of individuals coming together as peers in a spirit of kindness and open reciprocity.

Among my research participants, one significant way in which individuals engage is through a wide variety of groups focusing on specific practices, ideas or activities. I will argue that these groups adhere well to the elements of the Communities of Practice theoretical model as set out by Etienne Wenger (1998). They are places where individuals practice together, share ideas and cooperate in various ways, and their constitution varies in its level of formality. They are non-exclusive, non-dogmatic and avoid having clear doctrines. They tend to have loose and fuzzy boundaries, and are limited in their scope and in the expectations they make on members. Individuals claim the right to control their level of membership, and the profile and number of groups they join. Many such groups have limited duration, and there is consequently a dynamic cycling effect, whereby groups are formed, grow and then die – sometimes over a long period of time, but sometimes quickly. This enables individuals to learn, make contacts and then move on. The dual facts that individuals tend to be members of more than one group and that groups die and become replaced, together mean that individuals are able to get to know a large number of other individualized practitioners, and effectively become members of rich cultural networks, while also acting as connecting nodes within ongoing networks of groups.

Perhaps counterintuitively, the viability, richness and strength of this social environment depend on a shared notion of individuals as having authority over their own religious lives, as having their own subjective points of view, but as also being inclined towards sharing and collaborative behaviour. This constitutes an ideology of mutuality, whereby individuals are seen as independent but as naturally tending towards mutualized, caring and cooperative behaviour, and as seeking to empower one another rather than to dominate social situations. Individualized religion (in at least the forms and contexts exemplified by the population under study in this research) therefore represents a religious milieu that is theoretically distinct from, but every bit as functionally viable as, traditional institutional religion.

The social significance of individualized religious practice in this context consists in these groups and the wider networks, in that they provide a basis for rich, dynamic and ongoing social engagement. They are a significant social presence in and of themselves, and an important aspect of a wider creative and activist set of local subcultures. Moreover, they are a strongly contributing factor in maintaining the social cohesion of the local community, and in supporting the generation of collective activities and structures.

In this context, instead of objectivist transmission of dogma or doctrine, there is widespread transmission of ideas, practices, resources, interpretations and a host of other items of information. This occurs to a large extent within the many groups. They act as practice communities, forming a rich informational environment in which individuals share, but also work together to generate and develop religious content. This transmission is sometimes but by no means always verbal in nature. It also occurs through non-verbal cues, a variety of shared activities and other routes. Unlike the objectivist transmission of traditional hierarchical institutions, what is transmitted is only what is acceptable to its recipients, and is often developing and growing as well as being transmitted. The result is a strongly dynamic and vibrant environment. Transmission of the overall ideology of mutuality is also an ever-present and self-reinforcing undercurrent.

Note, however, that this argument is not intended as a refutation of the secularization thesis. I agree with the arguments put forward by Bruce and others as to the effect of individualization on many traditional and institutional forms of religion. However, it is also clear that extension of these arguments to individualized religious forms can fail to take full account of the structural ramifications of their subjective roots. As the research detailed in this book shows, there are highly plausible routes to social significance and onward transmission of individualized religion that are inherent in its subjective form. While this test case cannot be claimed as representative, it is indicative of a likelihood that such structures exist elsewhere, and that they have the capability of engendering social significant activity and of transmitting themselves and the content on which they predicate themselves over time. This work and the arguments that surround it therefore provide additional nuance to the secularization debate, by proposing new ways of theorizing individualized religion, new ways of thinking about the relationship between religious practitioners and the communities in which they involve themselves, and new ways of approaching the religious landscape post-secularization.

The research

There is a growing tradition of study of religion through the anthropological study of populations in local communities. While it cannot directly answer questions about the society-wide trends, this kind of study is useful in that it allows us to look in a holistic way at practitioners' lives, their social connections, their proximal practice communities and their wider social networks. Perhaps the most famous example of such a study is Paul Heelas and Linda Woodhead's comprehensive exploration of religious activity around Kendal (Heelas and

Woodhead, 2005). Heelas and Woodhead examined all instances of religious or spiritual activity they could identify in the area, categorizing them and assessing the relative prevalence of the different categories over a particular week (Heelas and Woodhead, 2005, 33–48). They then investigated the growth of what they called the holistic milieu through oral histories gained from interviews of individual participants (Heelas and Woodhead, 2005, 42–5). A number of such studies have focused on Glastonbury. Ruth Prince and David Riches (2000) looked at the New Age movement there, focusing on the community and social aspects particular to this location. They conceptualized the movement in Glastonbury in terms of communitas, drawing parallels with certain kinds of non-industrialized societies (Prince and Riches, 2000, 135, 214–32). Other important work in Glastonbury includes the work of Bowman (2013) and Redden (2005) (both are discussed in Chapter 2).

However, the specific nature of individualized religion suggests that a study focused on individuals as nodes in a network is likely to be more helpful than a traditional location study along these lines. For example, in preparing the ground for his study of the New Age, Steven Sutcliffe argues that its internal conversation tends to consist of 'a nexus of conversations, occasionally arguments, within a de-centred and theoretically unbounded matrix of viewpoints and pressure groups, here locally focused and there widely dispersed, but almost always mutually tolerant and hence diffusive rather than regulative' (Sutcliffe, 2003, 11). While Sutcliffe does acknowledge the significance of centres of activity and of co-located community (Sutcliffe, 2003, 150–4, 186–8), he is clear that 'the group is not the goal but a means to another, always deferred end' (Sutcliffe, 2003, 173), that end being individuals' personal and self-directed projects of seekership (Sutcliffe, 2003, 173, 200–8). Elsewhere, Sutcliffe highlights the need for 'more nuanced histories of the networks and enclaves of "alternative religion"' (Sutcliffe, 2014, 44). Similarly, in conceptualizing the New Age in terms of webs of interactions, Dominic Corrywright highlights the tensions inherent in attempts to centre study of this kind of activity on specific locations as well as the opportunity afforded by the tracing of non-localized connections (Corrywright, 2003, 112–13, 154–5, 159–61, 250–1).

While my research does centre itself and contextualize itself in a particular geographical area (Hebden Bridge), its methodological focus is on the understanding of associations, connections and networks specific to individuals under study over the development of a rounded understanding of those specific geographical areas of study in and of themselves. The aim is not to make conclusions about society-wide trends, but to examine the ways in which individuals who are practising in a subjectivized or individualized milieu think about and develop their own practice, and how they work with one another to construct their relational and associational forms, and to attempt to draw conclusions about the functional viability of this form of practice.

The structure of this book

As discussed earlier, this book combines a report on an ethnographic study of a particular population of individualized religious practitioners with the development of a theoretical model of individualized religion. Chapter 2 lays some theoretical groundwork through a critical discussion of some of the ways individualized religious practitioners have been theorized and of some theoretical considerations that should be taken into account when considering individualized religion. It begins by discussing individualization and secularization, specifically accounts of how individualization, together with rationalization, functional differentiation and privatization, has led in modernized societies to the decline of the social significance of traditional religious institutions, alongside declines in religious affiliation, practice and belief. The chapter goes on to consider some alternative models of secularization. A common theme of these is to problematize the thesis of overall unidirectional decline, instead arguing for more complex and contextually sensitive interactions between secularization processes. Of especial interest are those scholars who more clearly argue for a picture of change, especially where this involves transformation into less institutionalized forms. Grace Davie's model of believing without belonging (Davie 1994, 107–10) depends on a shifting of authority over what are acceptable beliefs and levels of involvement from the institution to the individual. Individuals feel free to utilize institutions' physical and conceptual resources but take personal control over how they do this. Paul Heelas and Linda Woodhead's subjective-life model (Heelas and Woodhead, 2005, 3–5) lays emphasis on subjectivity – on living one's religious life primarily according to one's own subjective experiences and needs. One line of critique against this notion of subjective-life spirituality is to argue that it is structurally nonviable, the most meticulously argued of such critiques being that of Bruce (2011, 112–19) as discussed earlier. Here I further develop my argument that critiques such as this that are developed from consideration of decline of traditional religious institutions are less well suited to the different ways social engagement and transmission would be likely to occur in a subjectivism-inspired milieu.

Chapter 2 then goes on to consider some other ways in which individualized religion has been theorized, focusing on notions of postmodernism and consumerization, and on the degree of social embeddedness of the individual. These discussions, and the theorizations that underpin them, are crucial to forming a rounded understanding of individualized religious practitioners and their capability to form religious community. The key point of this section follows Matt Dawson (2012) in identifying two categories of accounts of individualization. In the first, individualization is reported as socially disembedded, leading to a tendency for individuals to become atomized consumers. These consumers have an illusion of free choice, but in fact are limited by the range of stimuli and choices that are available. Both Craig Martin (2014) and Jeremy Carrette and Richard King (2005) provide convincing accounts of this kind of individualization. Dawson's alternative category of accounts of individualization, however, picks out the possibility of practice being both individualized and at the same time highly socially embedded. As the accounts of Gauthier, Redden, Bowman and others suggest, this kind of individualization is characterized by a shift from compliance to commitment, from consumerism to being an active, engaged and self-directed producer of one's own religious experience.

In order to better understand embedded individualization and the relationship with subjectivity, Chapter 2 then goes on to develop a theoretical framework for consideration of socially embedded individualized religion, based on a theory of the subject that affords the individual the capability to pick out both itself and its interlocutory peers as centres of subjective experience and agency, and underwrites the development of relations of meaningful engagement, cooperation and creativity. The chapter finishes by briefly re-engaging with the discussions around secularization and consumer religion in the light of this model, to suggest that socially embedded individualized practitioners may have routes to social significance and transmission that are not only rooted in their individualized status but dependent upon it.

Chapter 3 focuses on the local community around Hebden Bridge and the Upper Calder Valley, where the research on which this book is based took place. It begins with a potted history of the area up to and including the 1960s, which suggests a background of constant social change due to industrialization and subsequent de-industrialization, and a longstanding history of political and religious dissent. The next section focuses on the so-called hippy influx of the 1970s, which refers to the arrival of a wave of students and other young people with left-libertarian anti-authoritarian views. This new population was attracted by the cheap post-industrial housing, the beauty of the local area and a growing local counterculture. They brought with them idealistic notions of pioneering new and alternative lifestyles, politics and spiritualities, which have had a significant impact on local culture. Many of the participants in the current research are members of this generation, and still carry its ideals to varying extents. Since the 1970s there have been further waves of incomers, both attracted by and reinforcing the area's reputation as a centre of creative, socially innovative and politically radical activity. However, at the same time there has been a tendency towards commodification and gentrification of the area, which have fed off but also diluted this reputation. Some participants therefore talk of Hebden Bridge as having lost some of its character, and some of its radical edge. The chapter also goes on to discuss some of the social pressures that exist in the local area today. These include generational pressures, pressures of economic and social inequalities and environmental pressures due to the geographical nature of the area. While the town and valley are not perhaps the utopian idyll of the tourist brochures, there remains a local culture of left-libertarianism and a significant population of local people who engage in various forms of alternative religious practice in an individualized way. They constitute a vibrant local culture of non-institutionalized religiosity that forms an important aspect of the area's creative and cultural life. On the face of it at least, they appear to involve themselves in numerous groups, and other shared and collaborative activities, and so are a population with a relatively high likelihood of demonstrating the forms of socially embedded individualized religious activity that are of interest in this research.

Chapter 4 takes a step further in, to focus on the various subcultures, groups and other forms of engagement in which this population participates. The primary foci at this stage are first to form a picture of the wide diversity of beliefs, practice and affiliations among this population, but second to begin to develop an understanding of what patterns exist in participants' overall attitudes and engagements that might provide a basis for commonality and social linkage. The chapter begins by discussing general attitudes among the participants towards the idea of individualized practice. There is a general positive feeling towards the idea of so-called 'pick-and-mix' religion – a stance of claiming individual freedom to choose at a granular level what elements to incorporate into one's religious life. To varying degrees, participants tend to have their own personal religious practices. However, at the same time there is a widespread tendency to take part in a wide range of shared and collaborative activities.

The bulk of Chapter 4 focuses on four religious centres of gravity, each of which commonly arise in discussions of the individualized religious activity of participants. These are Quakerism, non-aligned Buddhism, nature-based and animistic religion, and Goddess and women's spirituality. They are probably best thought of as overlapping religious subcultures. These centres of gravity vary widely in their de facto patterns regarding affiliation, engagement and practice. However, there is also significant crossover between them, with many participants cleaving to more than one. It is important to note that all four of these are religious environments that explicitly value subjectivity and the placing of authority at the level of the individual. This also means that individuals who take part in each of the four decide for themselves the place and extent that it has in their personal religion. Each of the four also contains a circulating corpus of ideas and practices, which are again available for utilization as individuals see fit. These four centres of gravity are not the only religious subcultures that exist around Hebden Bridge, but they are simply the ones that are most popular among my participants.

In addition to the four centres of gravity, Chapter 4 charts the existence of loosely constituted informal practice groups. These tend to be based around shared participation in particular activities, have open and often revolving membership, and often tend to exist for finite periods of time. The groups picked out for description are significant only in that they are currently well attended by my participants. However, they are also exemplary of an ongoing and dynamic ecosystem of groups that rise and fall over time.

Having set the scene in Chapters 3 and 4, the next two chapters go on to do the theoretical heavy lifting work. Chapter 5 focuses in on individuals, while Chapter 6 looks in more detail at groups and other forms of engagement. Chapter 5 begins by examining the attitudes of participants towards religion and spirituality in more detail. They generally hold a deep antipathy to traditional religious institutions, connecting these with top-down hierarchy, dogma, doctrine and fundamentalism – all of which may be summed up in a perception that they disempower the individual. Most participants prefer to talk about what they do as spirituality, since this evokes for them a sense of connectedness and an exploratory, learning-focused approach to matters of belief and practice, while avoiding connotations of religious institution, dogma and hierarchy. The next section focuses on participants' notions of self and their underlying theories of the subject. The first and perhaps most important point here is the emphasis that participants place on the importance of their status as individuals who are in sole charge of their own religious lives. Whatever the degree to which this is borne out in practice, the fact that they frame this as such a high priority is of significance in its own right, and underpins the ways in which they work together to organize their mutual engagement and transmission practices. It is often expressed in tandem with advocacy of left-libertarian social and political views (sometimes including anarchism).

In their discourse and in their behaviour, participants utilize three distinct notions of self. First, as touched on earlier, they frame the self as a rational and free agency-bearing entity. This carries with it a sense of an element of choice. Second, participants posit the existence of an authentic, inner or ideal self. This carries a sense of being relatively unchanging, and of being something to be accessed, honoured or realized. Third, participants talk about the self as an experiencing entity, liable to be affected and even fundamentally transformed through its encounters. These three notions of self are clearly in some tension with one another, and not wholly compatible. However, participants shift between them easily and creatively in developing their understanding of their religious lives.

Chapter 5 then goes on to discuss knowledge, experience and belief. Participants tend to be antipathetic to the idea of belief, in part because they associate it with notions of doctrine and dogma, but also because they tend to prefer contingency with respect to propositions about themselves and about religion. Of course this does not mean they do not have beliefs, and in fact there are particular beliefs that are common among the participants in this research, and especially within each of the particular identified centres of gravity. However, the emphasis that participants place on subjectivity of belief tends towards a stance that someone's beliefs tend to be the right beliefs for them, rather than being necessarily true in objective terms. This kind of subjectivized stance with respect to matters of religion is very common among the participants of this research.

The remainder of Chapter 5 considers how participants approach learning about religion, and religious creativity. Fundamental to participants' understanding of religion are notions of experimentation and exploration. This can be a matter of seeking and interpreting experiences as a way of finding out about oneself and about others. As such it can be a very deliberate process, sometimes backed up by active religious (or related) research. However, experimentation can also be about the seeking of experiences as a way of transforming the self, either in the immediate moment or as an ongoing project of change. The changes that are sought tend to be about making the self more sensitive, skilful and knowledgeable. Creativity is closely related, tending to involve transformations of the self as well as of something in the outside world, and so linking subjective transformation with creative action. It should be pointed out at this stage that both learning and creativity tend to utilize the three notions of self that are mentioned earlier, segueing and perhaps even flipping between them as required to allow the building of a personally meaningful religious practice.

Chapter 5 thus establishes how individuals understand themselves as the driver of their own religious lives, and how in practice they then tend to prioritize subjectivity over objectivity. Further, it is suggested that they view their religious lives as projects of experimentation, exploration and creativity. In order to achieve all of this, they veer between seeing themselves as freely active choice takers, as malleable experiencers that are continually transformed through encounter, and as having an authentic self that shapes their religious life. Chapter 6 builds on this portrait of individualized religious practice to explore how participants engage, how they learn from and teach one another, and how the structures through which they do these things are rooted in their understanding of their religion specifically as individualized. The chapter begins by looking at the ideal of connectivity and mutuality that exists among individualized practitioners in this context. This tends to be broadly based on a combination of factors – notably a feeling that working together improves the potency of religious practice in terms of its effects on the individual, a thought that connecting with others is a more natural, authentic way to behave and a consideration that empathy towards others is a morally appropriate way to behave. These factors accord with the three notions of self that are discussed in Chapter 5. Overall, the impulse to connect, collaborate and share is predicated on an understanding of oneself and one's fellow practitioners as equal but independent peers. That is to say, the feelings that are at the root of collaboration here are fed and supported by individualization.

Chapter 6 then goes on to discuss in further detail the practice groups that were earlier identified as a major vehicle of collaboration. These groups vary considerably in what practices, ideas or experiences they centre themselves on. What they have in common is that they are environments that enable people to come together to practice in a collaborative way. While each one is unique, they tend to display many of the characteristics of Etienne Wenger's Communities of Practice (1998). Groups tend to provide opportunity for sharing ideas, information and praxis, but also enable the development of meaning to occur as a shared endeavour. They tend to have open and non-exclusive memberships, and fuzzy and permeable boundaries. Each tends to have its own, shared pool of resources and tools (ranging from mutual practices to commonly held ideas and so on), but they seek to avoid prescribing beliefs or making explicit demands on their members. They are dynamic and often vibrant, but also tend to be limited in their scope and their duration. The finite but cyclical nature of these groups (i.e. that they tend to grow, die off and then often become replaced with something else) means the wider shared cultural environment is not bound by the limitations of the groups, leaders or structures that exist at any one time.

There then follows a discussion on leadership and power relations, including participants' attitudes towards spiritual teachers. While participants are very suspicious of hierarchy and concerned about issues of interpersonal power, they do not reject concepts of leadership in their entirety. Rather, they tend to place caveats on what kinds of leadership are seen as acceptable and helpful. These seek to empower the individual as an independent centre of subjectivity and self-authorization. While participants feel free to accept one another as leaders in particular circumstances, these are limited to particular situations and subject to the ongoing authorization of the led. Moreover, they often occur in contexts of wider reciprocity, whereby different individuals take on the power of leadership at different times. Participants tend to be aware of the potential arising of power imbalances in relationships, and to respond by removing themselves from those situations. While it would not perhaps be correct to say there are no possibilities for imbalances of power in interpersonal relations, it would also be correct to say that it is very important to participants to avoid such imbalances. Significantly, many explicitly connect this with politically left-libertarian or even anarchist views, or with an awareness of gender politics.

Chapter 6 concludes with a discussion of how individuals and groups exist as part of a networked religious subculture in the local community, and as elements in the building of community. Participants themselves use a range of metaphors to describe what is going on, but the general picture is one of multiple layers of social connection. Individuals build their own personal networks, but each also connects through a number of groups, thus existing as a node of connection between these various groups. Groups are centres of engagement, but also places where relationships are formed that transcend their own existence. The result is a local community that has a high degree of social cohesion. Specifically, religious groups and activities are only one aspect of a wider culture of individualized engagement that also includes creative, environmental, political and other spheres of activity, and that is characterized by crossover between different spheres. However, the place that individualized religious practice and engagement have in the local culture does suggest, in this community at least, not only that it is capable of having social and religious significance but that the social and religious significance it does have is largely predicated on and a result of its individualized nature.

Chapter 7 concludes the book by bringing together the analyses of the previous chapters to suggest a model of individualized religion that facilitates both socially significant engagement and ongoing religious transmission. The chapter goes on to discuss the importance of these findings in broader context, and to suggest directions for future study.

2

Theorizing individualized religion

The study of individualized religion is, at root, the study of religion-practising individuals, and how they relate to one another and to other entities of various kinds. Part of the purpose of this book is to advocate for, and to lay in place building blocks for, a greater emphasis on anthropological study of the religious individual as an entity in its own right. In doing so I start from a perception that much contemporary academic study of religion focuses on study of particular religious groupings, communities or affiliational structures, and on describing their practices, beliefs and forms of association. This is understandable since religion is such a social activity. And of course, this work is of immense value in charting, categorizing and understanding the various religious groups, and in providing means for (among other things) comparison between contexts, and social or historical explanations. However, ethnography and sociology that focuses on social structures is less clearly suited to providing a sound understanding of religion practised at the level of the individual and of religion-practising individuals themselves. When the focus of study is the group, denomination or community, there is a potential for that study to privilege the interests of the group over those of the individual. If groups (formally or informally) expect and advocate specific patterns of belief or practise from their adherents, these could be reported as if they are the beliefs and practices of the individual members of the groups. Moreover, by focusing on the way that members of specific extant groups think and behave and engage, the student risks treating those patterns as if they have a greater universality than is really the case, and missing aspects of their inherent conditionality. This danger is magnified either if there are multiple groups that exhibit similar patterns to one another or if certain kinds of patterns are given validation by prevailing cultural or national hegemonies. There is then the further danger of reinforcing those hegemonies or of too readily dismissing alternative or novel patterns of belief or association.

Bruno Latour expressed these kinds of concerns well in his justification of his rejection of the 'sociology of the social' as his domain of study. As Latour states (2005, 11, emphasis is author's own),

> It's true that in most situations, resorting to the sociology of the social is not only reasonable, but also indispensable, since it offers convenient shorthand to designate all the ingredients *already accepted* in the collective realm. . . . But in situations where innovations proliferate, where group boundaries are uncertain, when the range of entities to be taken into account fluctuates, the sociology of the social is no longer able to trace actors' new associations. . . . (I) t is no longer enough to limit actors to the role of informers offering cases of well-known types. You have to grant them back the ability to make up their own theories of what the social is made of.

Latour is here speaking to a need to understand the individual as an entity that is not distinct from its engagement with other entities, and therefore (crucially) to avoid prejudging either the form of the individual as an entity or the nature of its relations with others. Taking this thought seriously, an approach is needed that roots itself in the individual's experience of others, its status as a being capable of performing actions in the world, and the ways in which the former informs the latter. Latour's formulation of Actor-Network Theory (ANT) (Latour, 2005) tries to do just that, in predicating itself on the notion that an individual's actions are rooted in the actions of other entities (or actors) on the individual concerned and seeking to understand the individual's behaviour in terms of those of its co-actors. The individual is seen as an entity that faces the world through engagement in relationships of dynamic mutuality with other entities, through which meaning is exchanged and constructed. The tracing of the influences on the individual of other actors is a way to situate and gain insights into its own actions, and crucially into its social situation (Latour, 2005, 30). This constitutes in effect advocacy of the value of what might best be thought of as a specifically subject-centred kind of ethnography.

ANT works from the intuition that the most meaningful way to understand the social is to trace the associations of individual 'actors', rather than to accept and work with any assumed social structures (Latour, 2005, 3, 5 and 247). This approach views social structures as uncertain, contingent and constantly shifting (Latour, 2005, 27–42 and 87–120), and views individual agency as causally embedded in the myriad influences of other actors (Latour, 2005, 43–62). Significantly, this set of actors is not restricted to human equivalents but can include the agency of a range of other entities including (for example) the narrative constructions of the actor under study, and non-human objects that are perceived as having had influence on their actions (Latour, 2005, 47–8 and 63–76). ANT views macro levels of association not as overarching levels of reality but simply as additional local actors. Instead of explanations in terms of obvious influencers, it looks out for multiple influences within the actors' orbit (Latour, 2005, 173–218). Finally, ANT methodologically views its own accounts not as objective reports about what is going on but as subjectively written texts – stories – which capture as well as possible the richness and range of associations of the actors under study, while at the same time recognizing their own inherent artificiality (Latour, 2005, 122–40).

As suggested by Corrywright (2003, 82), the holistic nature of web-type networks means that they do not have a single point of entry and can be investigated using multiple methods. Mika Lassander argues that ANT provides an open-ended methodology for exploring the complex intertwining of actors in vernacular religion, since religion, spirituality and society are seen not as pre-existing kinds of things but only as assemblages of actors. Lassander argues this avoids the privileging of specific predefined social structures (Lassander, 2012, 247–9). Similarly, Julian Holloway (2000) has argued that ANT is an especially useful tool in analysing interactions within the New Age, as it can take particular account of their dynamic and multivariate nature.

The purpose of this chapter is to set in place a theoretical framework to underpin the study of the religious individual as an entity in its own right, initially for use in the current research, but that also can be used more generically for work on religious individuals and their communities. I will start by considering secularization as a recent debate to which the status of religious individuals is key, and then go on to discuss the individual in postmodernist thought with particular emphasis on notions of consumer religion. Utilizing points from each of these discussions, I will go on to construct an overall theory framework, finishing with some notes about how it can be used.

Secularization and the individual

In the UK (as in other Western European countries), there is evidence of a decline over the last seventy or so years in the societal importance of the traditionally dominant Christian denominations, together with a decline in regular figures of attendances at Christian services and certain other indicators of participation (Bruce, 1996, 29–32; Bruce, 2003, 54–5). While the extent of decline and how these indicators should be interpreted are both contested (see, for example, Brown, 2009, 2–3), there clearly is a process of change that requires explanation. The theories of Durkheim and Weber have often been utilized in the interpretation of this process of change, especially in linking the decline of religion to processes of modernization (Warner, 2010, 26). Both of these provide potentially valuable insights into the relationships between religious individuals and their communities.

While Durkheim did acknowledge the existence of forms of religion freely constructed by each individual based on their own conscience and subjective states (Durkheim, 2001, 44–5), he argued that religion is ultimately communal in nature, and performs a function in society of maintaining social cohesion through its tendency to embed individuals within social networks based on common beliefs and practices (Durkheim, 2001, 46, 310–14; Durkheim, 2014, 131, 141). Over time, however, societies tend to become increasingly individualized, as collective representations are unable to contain individual sentiments. This results not only in the loss of community structures within society but also in the broadening, weakening and destabilizing of religion itself (Durkheim, 2014, 132–3). For Durkheim, Protestantism's particular emphasis on the individual has further reduced social cohesion, effectively accelerating this process (Durkheim, 1951, 124–5).

Also focusing on the effects of Protestantism, Weber emphasized the role of rationalism in causing the disenchantment of society (Weber, 2009, 281). He theorized this as occurring together with the growth of a secular and capitalistic economic rationality, as a consequence of Protestantism's conception of individual calling as ascetic worldly duty (Weber, 2012a, 95–116). In a separate but parallel argument, Weber identified a tendency in the evolution of organizations, including religious ones, towards more rationalized forms, which has the effect of defining and therefore restricting individual action (Weber, 2012b, 262).

Three further themes that often appear in accounts of secularization are functional differentiation, privatization of religion and religious pluralism. Functional differentiation is a posited shift, from a past society in which religion was treated as universally authoritative and relevant, to a society in which religion is seen as only one among many specialist and functionally isolated areas of expertise, causing religion also to lose its role as universal moral arbiter (Warner, 2010, 26–7; 31–2). Religion thus becomes privatized, in that it moves away from being a matter of public importance appropriate to the involvement of officialdom, towards becoming a matter of private individual conviction and choice (Warner, 2010, 27). As it becomes increasingly acceptable for individuals to make their own decisions about religious matters, a plurality of religious choices emerges, which (according, for example, to the early writings of Peter Berger) leads to a reduction in the plausibility of religious views, a neutralizing of religious claims, and an increase in relativism. All of these are understood to further undermine the importance of religion (Bruce, 2001, 88–9; Berger, 2012, 137–8). It is worth pointing out, however, that Berger later changed his view, arguing instead that pluralism widens the range of plausible views, increasing choice, and thus subjectivizing religion and giving more power to individual adherents (Berger, 2014, 17–49).

From the mid-twentieth century, these building blocks were brought together and developed into a coherent paradigm, sometimes known as 'Classical Secularization Theory' (Warner, 2010, 33), or the 'Standard Model of Secularization' (Martin, 2005, 123). Secularization was thus set up as a process whereby religions tend to lose their social significance under certain kinds of conditions (Wilson, 1982, 149). Bryan Wilson presented this process as inevitable, unidirectional and irrevocable (Wilson, 1982, 151, 154, 179). He argued that as local communities give way to complex industrial society, and as rationalization takes hold, religion's public role becomes increasingly marginalized and privatized. The effects of this include erosion of its status as provider of society's underlying normative moral framework, and the takeover of previously religious responsibilities by secular institutions (Wilson, 1982, 158, 159,162; Wilson, 2001). While not necessarily becoming completely extinct, religion undergoes significant decline in adherents to become only one of many competing privatized providers of meaning (Wilson, 1982, 154, 162, 176), and people increasingly act as 'anonymous individuals' (Wilson, 2001, 46).

Steve Bruce (2011, 57–78) gives a similar picture but further emphasizes the complexity of how parallel processes of individualism, social and structural differentiation and rationalization can mutually reinforce one another to bring about a decline in the social significance of religion, together with a decline in adherence and in the significance of religion to individual people's lives. Also prominent in Bruce's account is a sense that decline plays out over successive generations, through the impact of the individualization of one generation's religious practices on the level of take-up of the next.

Broadly speaking, the classical model of secularization theory centres on the decline of formerly prominent Christian traditions' and institutions' positions of authority and influence in society as a whole and in people's lives, as traditions become marginalized due to societal structural differentiation, as their conceptual frameworks are undercut by increasing rationalization, and as individuals become ever more empowered to make their own choices rather than being led by their religious leadership. For Wilson, even religious revivals are part of this process of secularization, since their attempts to create islands of religious authority are ultimately privatizing and individualizing acts, which therefore contribute to a widening climate of divergence of opinion and affiliation (Wilson, 1982, 152–3).

José Casanova (2006, 7–8) has argued that functional differentiation, the privatization of religion and the decline of religious beliefs and practices should all be treated (analytically and empirically) independently from one another. He urges us to move away from the idea that these factors combine to make a predictable direction of travel, instead suggesting they interact with one another in complex ways to produce diverse patterns of secularization that differ according to societal context. He argues that comparative historical analysis is necessary to elucidate the seemingly very different trajectories occurring in various contexts (Casanova, 2006, 8 and 11). While in Europe all three factors perhaps appear to have occurred together, Casanova argues that in the US differentiation has not historically been accompanied by privatization or the decline of belief and practice to the same degree (Casanova, 2011, 60). He goes on to argue that the view that modernity entails individualism and rationality at the expense of community is over-simplistic, instead claiming that in such an environment there are expanded possibilities for new kinds of voluntary religious association (Casanova, 2006, 18).

Similarly, Karel Dobbelaere (2007, 137) has argued that secularization can be broken down into three sub-components: individual secularization, organizational secularization (which relates to the rationalization and bureaucratization of religious institutions and organizations; Dobbelaere, 2002, 35–8) and societal secularization (which refers to replacement of an overarching religious cosmos with political and secular ideologies, in a process broadly equivalent to that of functional differentiation; Dobbelaere, 2002, 29). For Dobbelaere, the concept of 'individual secularization' does not correspond to decline of religious belief and practice per se, but to loss of the control of these by various religious authorities (Dobbelaere, 2007, 139). He thus defines a secularized society as one in which religion has been privatized and functionally differentiated, but in which there still exists a latent religiosity among individuals. Formerly dominant religious institutions are still able to compete to cater for this, alongside other providers of meaning (Dobbelaere, 2007, 144). Thus for Dobbelaere, as for Casanova, the process of secularization is not unidirectional but involves complex interaction between different non-dependent elements. Both the trajectory and the endpoint are therefore contingent and in need of empirical testing (Warner, 2010, 56), and the study of religion should really now be transcended by a wider study of meaning systems (Dobbelaere, 2014, 219).

Both Casanova and Dobbelaere suggest that continued decline of religiosity is not inevitable. Rodney Stark goes further in arguing that a past 'Age of Faith' never really existed, and that in both medieval and early modern times mass participation in and understanding of Christianity were no greater than they are today (Stark, 1999, 253–6). Stark argues that a potential demand for religion exists relatively constantly in all cultures (irrespective of the effects of modernization), which awaits activation by religious suppliers (Stark, 1999, 263 and 269). Elsewhere, with William Bainbridge, Stark elaborates this rational-choice approach by examining the so-called supply side of religion more closely (Stark and Bainbridge, 1985). Stark and Bainbridge argue for a cyclical process of the birth, transformation and decline of particular suppliers of religion (Stark and Bainbridge, 1985, 2), as they progress from being entrepreneurial and innovative cults in tension with the wider culture to becoming 'respectable', in low tension with wider culture but bureaucratic and suppressive of innovation, and thus liable to decline and replacement by newer forms better able to tailor themselves to meet demand (Stark and Bainbridge, 1985, 2–3, 432–6). Stark and Bainbridge thus see religious change as due to change in the structures of religious organizations (echoing Weber, but very much as a cyclical process), and the decline of certain kinds of religion in modern Europe as an effective – and self-limiting – clearing away of a barrier to future religious vitality (Stark and Bainbridge, 1985, 2).

Steve Bruce argues against this kind of supply-side model, using various statistical data to convincingly show that far from creating greater religious participation, religious diversity (taken as an indicator of the existence of religious innovation and entrepreneurial activity) tends to lead to a reduction in participation in extant religious institutions (Bruce, 2011, 143–7). However, it should also be pointed out that the data discussed by Bruce tend to refer to membership and attendance in traditional Christian denominations that in this context would be declining hegemonic suppliers rather than innovative new suppliers. Perhaps on a fair reading of Stark and Bainbridge's position, regrowth (if it does occur) might well also be expected to occur elsewhere and look and feel significantly different, precisely because the emergent forms are defined as innovative. A perhaps more trenchant criticism of Stark and Bainbridge's economics-led approach is the claim of Gauthier et al. (2013, 7–8) that it is inappropriately reductionist with respect to the needs and desires of individuals, and thus does not take account of the complexity or diversity of their various religious responses.

David Martin has also sought to problematize the idea of a unidirectional theory of secularization (Martin and Catto, 2012, 374). While accepting that religion in Britain has suffered a loss of its 'sacred aura' and 'cultural monopoly' (Martin and Catto, 2012, 386), Martin argues that the interactions between religion and society are necessarily complex, and contingent on factors specific to particular cultural, religious and national contexts (Martin, 2005, 55). Therefore, they cannot be regarded as 'a single track to a common terminus' (Martin, 2005, 47). He makes use of a historical argument that successive waves of Christianization and secularization have occurred in various European countries as a dialectic between the Christian tradition and evolving cultural contexts, in an ongoing and specifically Christianized regional cultural history (Martin, 2005, 78–85; Martin and Catto, 2012, 385–7). Thus, Martin presents secularization due to modernity as part of a wider picture of religious change brought about by the rise and fall of successive institutions (Martin, 2005, 3). Steve Bruce responds by accepting that the history of Christianity in Europe might not be a steady linear decline, but arguing that Martin's waves of Christianization, to the extent that they do occur, are likely to have successively less power and influence over time as the forces of secularization have their inevitable and ongoing effect (Bruce, 2011, 6).

Various authors have argued that while modernity (and most especially its associated processes of individualization) may have led to the decline of traditional religious forms and institutions, this is most accurately portrayed as a process of change rather than one of decline. Grace Davie, for example, argues that the decline in empirical indicators of commitment to religious institutions and of religious practice (e.g. attendance) is not reflected in indicators of people's subjective beliefs and values (Davie, 2006, 275; Davie, 2015, 5). She goes on to suggest that a significant proportion of the population may continue to harbour some level of (albeit divergent) belief, famously coining the phrase 'believing without belonging' (Davie, 1994, 107 and 194; Davie, 2015, 78–9). She argues that these believers may still take vicarious benefit from the continued existence of religious institutions (Davie, 2006, 277–81; Davie, 2015, 81–3), but define their own levels of involvement based on personal choice rather than any kind of sense of obligation (Davie, 2006, 281–4; Davie, 2015, 160).

David Voas and Alasdair Crockett argue in response to Davie that the data show no significant discrepancy between belief and affiliation or attendance

(Voas and Crockett, 2005, 13). They point to empirical studies showing that levels of transmission of general religiosity and of specific affiliation from parents to their offspring roughly correspond, suggesting generational decline of both (Voas and Crockett, 2005, 21–3), and that, where it does exist, belief without belonging merely constitutes 'undisciplined and possibly transitory supernaturalism' without personal or social significance (Voas and Crockett, 2005, 25). Voas and Crockett are right to suggest that there is no evidence to support a simple transition to a society of fairly orthodox but independent Christian believers, as Davie is quick to agree (Davie, 2015, 79). However, Voas and Crockett's objection also relies on the untested assumption that the kind of radical divergence of belief and practice suggested by the phrase 'undisciplined supernaturalism' can lead only to forms of religiosity that are insignificant and unworthy of serious consideration. If we are to take seriously the possibility that new or different forms of religion may be occurring that lay greater emphasis on individual subjectivity, then there is a need to more fully understand how these might exist, function and express themselves prior to any attempt at evaluation of their prevalence or their social or personal significance.

Based in part on Paul Heelas's earlier model of 'self-spirituality' as (in part) dependent on relationality (e.g. Heelas 1996, 27, 33), the Kendal study of Heelas and Linda Woodhead focuses on the question of whether traditional associational religious forms and denominations are in the process of being replaced in society by more individualized forms of spirituality. Heelas and Woodhead argue that there is an increasing emphasis on individual 'subjective-life', identifying this as a significant attractor to New Age spiritualities (Heelas and Woodhead, 2005, 7 and 10), and linking it to a cultural shift in society towards living life according to one's own subjective experiences and needs (Heelas and Woodhead, 2005, 2). Similarly, while acknowledging that personal religiosity has always been a 'highly individual collage of beliefs and practices' even in what are thought of as the more monolithic traditions (Bowman, 1999, 182), Marion Bowman has argued that individuals involved in New Age spiritualities feel especially free to talk about their own personal beliefs in the context of a relativistic approach to spiritual truths that validates and values individuals' own personal versions of truth (Bowman, 1999, 182). This individualized kind of approach to religion is identified by various authors as key to the New Age (e.g. Harvey and Vincett, 2012, 158), and often cited as occurring alongside a lack of centralized institutional control (e.g. Redden, 2005, 232).

Steve Bruce is among those who are sceptical of the power of 'subjective-life' spirituality to sustain itself over successive generations (e.g. Bruce, 2003, 61).

As discussed in the previous chapter, he argues that as religion becomes more individualized it becomes harder to maintain commitment, since there is no 'external power that the group can mobilize to press the weaker members to do what is right' (Bruce, 2011, 114). Consensus becomes difficult to maintain without recourse to coercion, which in turn mitigates against successful cooperative action (Bruce, 2011, 114), and the eclecticism of the individualized milieu leads to a lack of cohesion in which elements of religions become removed from their spiritual content, co-opted and trivialized (Bruce, 2011, 116–17). Finally, he argues that because there is no commonly accepted set of religious truths, there is no inherent impetus to evangelize (Bruce, 2011, 117–18). Bruce argues that these structural features are inherent to individualized religion because of its individualized nature, and that they tend to mitigate both against socially significant practice and against transmission (especially intergenerational transmission) (Bruce, 2011, 19, 117–18). As discussed in the previous chapter, the applicability of this argument to this kind of subjectivity-led practice is the crux of the matter of the social significance of individualized religion. Before summarizing the reasons why I think this argument is poorly applicable to this kind of activity, I must first prepare the ground by further exploring theories of subjectivity and of the subject and their specific importance to discussions about individualized religion.

Postmodernism and consumer religion

Individualized religion is sometimes framed as a phenomenon of postmodernity – that is of a world in which objectivity and hierarchy have been eroded, leaving a multiplicity of meaning generating agencies whose claims to superiority can only be made in pragmatic terms (Baumann, 1992, 35). David Lyon, for example, argues that postmodernity contributes to a 'fragmentation of institutional structures and intellectual belief systems', which individuals then seek to restructure in novel and diverse ways (Lyon, 2000, 54). Elsewhere he describes this in terms of the emergence of a 'cultural marketplace' where a consumerized attitude to cultural and social life predominates, identifying New Age spirituality as a prime exemplar of this trend (Lyon, 2000, 75). This potentially echoes both Davie's emphasis on a move towards personal choice and Stark's rational-choice model. However, it's important to be careful when considering religion in terms of consumerism and marketplaces, since there are multiple ways in which this can be (and indeed has been) operationalized, and these can lead to very different conclusions about individualized religion and its practitioners.

One kind of perspective sees consumer religion primarily as a phenomenon of capitalist society and ideology. Jeremy Carrette and Richard King, for example, focus on the buying and selling of religion-related product as a profit-generating exercise (whether explicitly or otherwise). They argue that religion has been rebranded in a kind of 'silent takeover', such that the 'dominant discourse of spirituality' is now grounded in what they call the 'modern capitalist ideology of individualism' (Carrette and King, 2005, 20-1, 29, 180), thus closely aligning individualism with capitalist consumerism. They go on to argue that underlying this is a form of psychological individualism that 'over-indulges ideas of an isolated self to the detriment of social interdependence', and that private consumer spirituality offers meaningless values that serve only to mask the 'oppressive and abusive mechanisms of global corporate power' (Carrette and King, 2005, 56-8). Craig Martin goes further in analysing how this kind of discourse supports capitalism. He argues that the theoretical concept of individual and personalized religion is a false one, which creates and sustains an illusion of religious autonomy. This enables people to feel as if they are acting as individuals, while actually accommodating to and thus legitimizing and perpetuating capitalist norms (Martin, 2014, 74-5). Martin claims that in popular discourse, 'institutional' religion thus becomes synonymous with 'bad' religion. This kind of attribution is often applied to religion that restricts full participation in capitalist consumer society, while religion that allows full participation is labelled 'individual' or 'spirituality', and thereby seen as acceptable (Martin, 2014, 68-74). Religious individualism is thereby reduced to the 'pursuit of distinction via the consumption and display of consumer goods' (Martin, 2014, 155). To focus on individual choice as a locus of meaningful religion is thus to ignore, or even mask, the structural realities of capitalist society (Martin, 2014, 155).

Matt Dawson identifies views such as Martin's as forming a category of critiques that place individualization 'within the broader political context of neoliberal societies' (Dawson, 2012, 311). This kind of view sees individualization as a false illusion of autonomy, where free choice is valorized but enabled only within a set of socially acceptable 'responsible' consumer options. While appearing diverse, these in practice confine individuals' field of action, ensuring compliance by 'individualizing failure', and thus ultimately serving the needs of neoliberal capitalism (Dawson, 2012, 311-12). For Martin, individualized religion is no more or less than a particular subset of these consumer options. The examples he uses to back up his case are novels, self-help books, fashion items and other consumer products, primarily produced by capitalist enterprises for a broad-based consumer market, and it is not surprising that these appear to support this kind of view. However, this is not the full story. As Dawson suggests, even if one accepts that individualization as brought about by consumerism and neoliberal social structures generally serves to make behaviour predictable, there is evidence that this is then susceptible to subversion as individuals become increasingly critical of their situation (Dawson, 2012, 311–12).

An alternative perspective is exemplified by François Gauthier et al. (2013), who see consumer religion primarily in terms of what they call a 'primacy of authenticity'. This, they argue, has the power to effect a transformation from compliance to commitment, as individuals become empowered to make their own judgements regarding religious truth (Gauthier et al., 2013, 15). Furthermore, and importantly, they caution against a simplistic understanding of markets in terms of supply and demand, suggesting that they are better seen as 'networked and hyper-mediatized arenas of mutual exposure' (Gauthier et al., 2013, 18). Gauthier et al. do, however, conceptually link consumer religion with consumer society, seeing brands as the symbols around which social relations form themselves, and commoditization as the circulation of these symbols to produce and reproduce meaning and value (Gauthier et al., 2013, 18). Similarly, in his discussion of how corporate branding utilizes ritualization, George González goes further, arguing that religious studies and marketing share the same epistemic context and that religious studies would therefore benefit from 'recognizing that its own discourse does not escape the context of neoliberalism' (González, 2015, 11).

Guy Redden explicitly equates the idea of a spiritual marketplace with a literal marketplace of commercial transactions, arguing that it is the very dynamic of commercial exchange that provides the impetus for the circulation and dissemination of practices and ideas, and which thus ultimately also shapes them (Redden, 2005, 234–7, 241). For Redden this helps to explain the relativistic nature of the New Age (as an operating principle of the market) as well as its unboundedness (as stimulated by a business interest in creating new product) and its emphasis on therapy (as a kind of marketing hook) (Redden, 2005, 241–2). Redden is clear that the commercial market has not caused the New Age's emphasis on relativistic individualism, that he does not see the New Age as only a market and nothing else, and that to view the New Age in this way is not at all to imply that New Agers are frivolous, gullible or inauthentic (Redden, 2005, 243–4). However, he does claim that the market provides a commercialized space which allows individuals to freely choose their path, and that it thus further feeds the individualistic nature of the New Age (Redden, 2005, 241–2).

Marion Bowman notes the tendency among some authors to use terms like 'spiritual supermarket' and 'pick-and-mix' in a derogatory fashion, arguing that these terms should instead be seen as a neutral and useful way of characterizing a situation of greater consumer choice and availability (Bowman, 1999, 182). Focusing on holistic healing, Bowman notes the availability of a wide range of courses and books aimed at prospective practitioners, a growing emphasis on earned qualifications, and consequently an increasing convergence between professional and personal development (Bowman, 1999, 187–8). Significantly, however, Bowman also points out that the majority of consultants act as cottage industries with minimal profit, thus suggesting that these consultants' motives are primarily spiritual or personal rather than financial (Bowman, 1999, 188). Bowman also touches on the possibility of gender playing a part, noting that these practitioners are predominantly female.

Bowman identifies Glastonbury as a specialized geographical locus of spiritual consumption with a well-developed spiritual service industry, arguing that this does provide a geographical centre for the kind of market discussed by Redden (Bowman, 2013, 218). Bowman further highlights a complex relationship between notions of value, spirituality and the monetary costs attached by practitioners to products and services, such that these notions of value do not necessarily coincide (Bowman, 2013, 207). While Bowman broadly accepts Redden's model, she also points out that many of the spiritual suppliers at Glastonbury donate time and energy free for various initiatives, that many feel strongly about the importance of 'right livelihood', and crucially that they tend to see their relationship with other suppliers in terms of spiritual cooperation rather than commercial competition (Bowman, 2013, 220–2). Thus, while the notion of the marketplace does appear to be a useful concept in helping understand Glastonbury and the wider New Age, it does not tell the whole story, either about individuals' core motivations and self-identification as New Agers or about how they interact with one another to develop and inform their spiritual journeys. Similarly, Andrew Dawson argues that the New Age's explicit emphasis on the value of the inner self reinforces its 'anti-consumerist credentials', suggesting instead what he calls a 'mystical consumption' that tends to reduce the status of material wealth to that of an 'optional, although not unwelcome, extra' (Dawson, 2011, 312–13).

Adam Possamaï explores the commodification of culture by New Age, Pagan and other postmodern practitioners through the creation of products, services and printed material, and the consequent consumption of these by spiritual consumers. He argues that this kind of cultural consumption is wide ranging in scope, and crucially that it is ultimately a creative activity, which might involve transformations of meaning within the self or the justification of previously held beliefs (Possamaï, 2002, 197, 201, 214).

The ways in which these authors understand notions of consumer religion vary widely, and it is tempting to link these to the various contexts in which their research has been focused. For example, Carrette and King's notion of consumer religion relies heavily on a specific set of illustrative examples. Some are rogue traders like Stephen Russell (Carrette and King, 2005, 89–91), whose inclusion is used to suggest a widespread cynical manipulation of consumers by practitioners for their own personal gain. Others (e.g. M. Scott Peck; Carrette and King, 2005, 54–6) are portrayed as utilizing and commoditizing traditional religions in a way that is both superficial and encouraging of self-indulgence. In this use of example cases, Carrette and King undoubtedly demonstrate that fraudulent practitioners and/or superficial practice do exist. However, they do not demonstrate that these are either more prevalent in or representative of New Age spirituality than would be the case in older, more institutional forms of religion, or indeed in the religion of past times. Moreover, as argued by Paul-François Tremlett (2013, 467), to label a religion fake or otherwise inauthentic can be to wrongly privilege traditional notions of religion, and so to misunderstand or omit the ways in which these religions might function effectively. Because Carrette and King do not theorize their concepts of inauthentic religion, they fail even to demonstrate that these example cases lack value for their adherents.

Gauthier et al., Redden, Bowman and Possamaï are all careful to differentiate their discussions of consumer religion from those that accuse it of trivialization or inauthenticity, and indeed they do demonstrate how notions of consumer religion can be helpful in understanding aspects of New Age, individualistic and other forms of contemporary religion. Especially, they highlight the potential viability of contexts without membership commitment or prescribed truths that enable individuals to choose the level and terms of their own engagement. However, there are pitfalls in these accounts. First, discussions such as these can still tend (even inadvertently) to privilege analogy between these engagements and those between for-profit shareholder companies and their customers. An example of this is Gauthier et al.'s citation of Douglas Atkins' discussion of brands like Apple and Harley Davidson to exemplify a trend towards the 'culting of brands', whereby marketing is not only about selling but also about selling a sense of meaning, community and experience (Gauthier et al., 2013, 9). This comparison, and especially the stronger version put forward by González (2015), must be understood as imperfect at best, since shareholder-owned companies' use of values in their branding will necessarily be ultimately predicated on the maximization of profits for their shareholders, and not on the values themselves. The fact that corporate branding utilizes aspects of religion does not, therefore, imply that religion is like marketing. But second, however, any analyses positioning individualized religion specifically as consumer religion risk overlooking the distinction between cynical cultural appropriation and self-directed spiritual experiment. They also risk deprivileging the wider involvement that individualized religious practitioners might have in their local community, and its consequent impacts – a good example being the widely touted first Druid Mayor of Glastonbury in 2015 (Bowman, 2016). While it is useful to conceptualize postmodern religion as fragmented and under ongoing reconstruction by individuals existing in shared spaces where they can construct meaning and value and community for themselves, there is a need for theories that better understand the extent to which these individuals are embedded within their shared spaces, in their relationships with others and with the shared beliefs, artefacts and other resources with which they work.

Particularly useful in helping us make sense of this range of views is the above-mentioned analysis of Matt Dawson (2012), who reviews various critiques of individualization in the literature and identifies two differing categories of accounts. On the one hand are accounts of 'disembedded individualization', which is theorized in terms of the disappearing significance of social connections and increasing social isolation of the individual. Martin's account fits into this category since it represents an illusion of connectedness that both feeds and masks an increasing atomization of individuals, disembedding them from their communities. On the other hand, however, Dawson identifies accounts of 'embedded individualization', which is theorized primarily in terms of the privatization of concerns to the level of individual responsibility (Dawson, 2012, 313). This category might include the accounts of Bowman and Possamaï and suggests individuals with a 'reflexive awareness of individual responsibility', who are then capable of creating meaningful connection to form community. This kind of theorization allows for the possibility of religion that is individualized in the sense of prioritizing individual action, but that nevertheless admits of collective forms of identity and action (see Dawson, 2012, 310, 313–14).

The subject and subjectivity

A workable theory of individualized religion needs to be subject centred, in that it needs to facilitate explication of the implied special status of the individual.

It also needs to be relational, in allowing for evaluation and characterization of engagements between individuals. And finally it has to help us understand the transmission of ideas, beliefs and practices between individuals. In the next three sections I will examine each of these aspects in turn.

As I have already suggested, following Latour, to be subject-centred means to avoid prejudging the individual as an engaging being. Instead there is a need to accommodate the range of frameworks through which individuals might think of and theorize their own status as subjects, and to take seriously their subjective experiences of being affected and motivated by their encounters.

We have already seen how religious institutions can invoke supposedly objective religious truths and firm leadership to ensure compliance in group practice. Underlying this is a Cartesian framework of the self as an isolated reasoning being – the 'I' that is 'a substance of which the whole essence or nature consists in thinking' (Descartes, 1968, 54), and which is therefore susceptible to instruction through reason. This notion underpins strands of thought that have been prevalent in Western society since at least Augustine, that see the 'I' as functionally independent – the first cause of its own intentional actions (Boyne, 2001, xi). It is this kind of view of the subject that underpins rational-choice and market approaches, which view religion in terms of an array of products set before a supposedly discerning (or at least choosing) consumer (e.g. see Stark, 1999, 259).

An alternative framework is a phenomenological one, which acknowledges the individual as having privileged access to its own subjective viewpoint, but without necessarily requiring it to be treated as functionally independent. The individual is seen in terms of its subjective status as a being in the world that faces and is faced by things other than itself. Note that the level of granularity of the individual's experience of other is itself subjective and therefore also contingent. At one extreme it could be understood in terms of a holistic relationship with a single landscape of experience through which meaning is inferred (or, as it may appear to the subject, disclosed). Broadly this equates to Heidegger's concept of the Clearing (Heidegger, 2000, 214–15). At the other extreme, it could be understood as a multiplicity of relationships with other individualized entities, each of whom has discrete meaning discernible by the subject somewhere on a spectrum ranging (to borrow from Buber, 2004, 13–16), from 'I–It' type relationships (experiences of engagement with passive object), to 'I–Thou' relationships (as if with a peer in a relationship of direct mutuality such that the individual's being and actions are affected by those of their peer entities). In a manner analogous to Latour's ANT discussed earlier, this suggests a notion of the individual as an entity facing the world, engaging in relationships of affective dynamic mutuality, and exchanging and constructing meaning through those engagements.

It should be clear from this that the co-actors whose actions underlie those of the individual are not necessarily peers in the sense of being fellow humans. They are peers in the sense of being identifiable (by the individual and hence by the researcher) as nodes of effect-causing activity. Bearing in mind the argument for the contingency of granularity, it seems plausible to think of these not as isolated black boxes but as heterogeneous assemblages – what Bennett (2010, 23–4), following Deleuze and Guattari (2013), calls:

> ad hoc groupings of elements, of vibrant materials of all sorts. Assemblages are living, throbbing confederations that are able to function despite the persistent presence of energies that confound them from within.

Inherent in this idea of an assemblage is the underlying notion that the existence of the subject as an entity in its own right is bound up with its ability to function as a system – to act in some kind of coherent way, however loose, to produce an effect or set of effects. An assemblage would therefore survive changes in its constitution that do not end its ability to function as a system, but not those that do. That is to say that assemblages can have fluid compositions and fuzzy boundaries. They also do not need to be exclusive – an assemblage can plausibly contain other assemblages, or be contained within other assemblages, or have boundaries that cross over those of other assemblages. Its function as a system, and therefore its identity as an assemblage, can evolve as its composition and activity evolve. This way of thinking about individuals also bears some comparison to Marilyn Strathern's use of the term 'dividual' to denote an individual understood as a kind of social microcosm (quoted in Sahlins, 2011, 12).

A theory of the subject for the purposes of explicating individualized religion has to perform two key functions. First, it has to provide a coherent framework through which to understand the forms of engagement in play and how the subject might relate and act through these in a socially significant way. But also, it needs to allow for and incorporate the ways in which participants theorize their own selves, in order to demonstrate a link between their own frameworks and these forms of engagement. It therefore needs to be plausible in its own right, but also inclusive of a variety of elements, which might appear on the face of it inconsistent. To this end, my working model of the subject is based around a series of potential capabilities. The subject is understood as an entity that can have a phenomenologically distinct point of view, but without this necessarily corresponding to a fixed or firmly boundaried entity. It can relate to its outside world as to a shifting universe of assemblages upon which it can act and by which it can be acted upon. Rather than being functionally isolated, it can therefore act as a player within a wider landscape of cause and effect, its actions being rooted in the actions of other entities. Its composition is not fixed but can itself be seen as an assemblage. This means other entities can be contained within it or can cross over or straddle its boundaries. Its boundaries are indistinct, fuzzy and porous. Its identity as an entity can evolve dynamically as it relates to the outside world, as it acts and is acted upon, and as its composition changes. It can also participate in numerous assemblages and can engage with its outside world at various levels of granularity.

On this kind of theory of the subject, there is no functional difference between what it is to be an individual and what it is to be an assemblage. All individuals can potentially be thought of as (in some sense) systems – assemblages of any number of components that gain their status as individuals from their level of coherence and cohesion. At the same time all individuals can be thought of as also components of other assemblages that are themselves understandable as individuals. Each imaginable entity, then, is at the same time an individual, a potential component of any number of larger assemblages, and an assemblage composed of any number of components.

Focusing in on individualized religious practitioners as a subclass of the class of individuals called humans, this model enables their religious activity to be explored as a domain of activity that is meaningful from the point of view of the individual, and rooted in a dynamic relationship of engagement with other entities at all levels. It also provides tools for understanding the ways in which individuals' own notions of self may underpin socially significant engagement, without prejudging what those notions of self may be. Most importantly, it provides a framework that is inclusive of potentially contradictory models that individuals may hold about their own status.

It is also worth at this stage briefly clarifying the epistemological position of this research with respect to participants' expressed points of view and the ways they frame themselves and their religious lives. This research tackles the religious lives of participants from multiple angles, ranging from observations of their religion-related social activities to inferences about aspects of individuals' self-identity. While the former is a matter of straightforward observation, the latter is more problematic, as I am interested not only in participants' outward behaviour but also in how they frame that behaviour and how this relates to the social structures in which they participate.

Although my research subjects have some kind of privileged insight into how things seem from their own point of view, they are not necessarily reliable witnesses. Each will not have full access to the workings of his or her own being, since the natures of their relationships with their outside world, their psychologies and their awareness of their psychologies are complex, and not fully apparent to themselves. There is no reason to assume that, even to the extent that it does exist, my subjects' awareness of either their own psychology or their relationship with the social world exists in any form that is straightforwardly amenable to verbalization. In addition, there are myriad possibilities for self-deception, self-affirmation and a range of other tricks or games that the individual may play on her or his self. There is also of course always the potential for straightforward attempts to deceive me as a researcher for a variety of possible reasons. However, my intention was not to gain from participants a flawless account of their inner psychology and external relations. What I was interested in was how they present their framing of their individual selves in the expression of their religious practice (through analysing their verbal accounts of their religious lives), what culturally important notions of self are common in the discourse of the population as a whole, and how these ways of framing the individual inform and work alongside the forms of social engagement that occur in practice.

In finding out from individuals their framing of their religious selves and religious lives, I therefore do not rule out any possibility of deception, self-serving descriptions or plain error, and I attempt to keep alive to the possibility of these in my critical analysis. But at the same time I am aware that knowledge of an individual's viewpoint is situated in, and therefore specific to and limited by, the perspective of the individual claiming that knowledge (Haraway, 1988, 581). In the endeavour of seeking a reliable account of the subjects of my participants I am situated in my own perspective and do not necessarily have greater access to any underlying objective truth (whether or not such a thing exists). Instead I have sought to construct an account that is as plausible as possible for the purposes of this research. This is made much easier by the fact that I do not necessarily need to pronounce on the accuracy of their expressed self-perception of their motives and actions, since it is the way these are framed that is of interest to me. For example, if a number of individuals plausibly tell me that they wish to avoid imbalance of power relations in interpersonal discourse, and if groups are formed in which there is evidence of shared action to attempt to avoid hierarchical power relations, then it is plausible to posit a shared ideal that links back to how individuals frame their own situation in relation to power. This remains the case even if in practice some are more controlling of others than they may wish to admit. If their framing of the nature of their subject in their religious lives is deceptive, inaccurate or self-serving then that may be of interest in its own right, but for my purpose how they frame themselves remains of interest.

Relationality

A theory of individualized religion not only must provide a framework to understand the individual as a relational entity but also needs to provide resources to characterize the relational forms that arise from this. At the simplest level, we have already seen how individualized religion can be modelled as socially embedded or disembedded. Where the focus of research is specifically on (for example) the role of commercial spirituality-related product in the development of late capitalist society, then we tend to see accounts of disembedded individualization such as those of Martin and Carrette and King. Both these accounts describe how the forces of capitalism can serve to isolate and atomize individuals and their practices. However, as we have also seen, individualization need not entail disembeddedness. Indeed, models that include or allow for mechanisms of potential embeddedness within more localized community structures are likely to be of greater interest for the current purpose of investigating and theorizing functionally viable individualized religion. There are numerous contexts in the literature in which practitioners (religious or otherwise) are properly identifiable as individualized (according to the definitions discussed in the previous chapter), but where community remains a crucial part of the story. Useful frameworks for our purpose include gift economies, networked social movements and vernacular religion.

David Bollier characterized a gift economy as 'a web of enduring moral and social commitments within a defined community sustained through the giving of gifts . . . without any assurance of personal return' (Bollier, 2013, 30). The concept has been used in recent times to help explain, for example, spontaneous grassroots projects such as New York's Community Gardens (Bollier, 2013, 16–18), and the rise of the open source software development movement (Raymond, 1999, 80–2; Bollier, 2013, 27–30). In his discussion of cooperation between open source software developers, Eric S. Raymond (1999) makes an analogy to a 'babbling bazaar of differing agendas and approaches', where the primary mode of exchange is through sharing, and status is afforded not through formal hierarchies but dynamically as a result of good peer reputation

(Raymond, 1999, 21, 81 and 85). In this environment, the cooperative task of building something that participants feel matters can be a significantly more important driver than monetary transactions or financial gain. While individuals may each have their own personal motivations and agendas, they are able to come together in cooperation by developing a shared creative space to which individuals choose to contribute. The concept of a cooperation-based gift economy coheres well with, for example, Adam Possamaï's concept of affinitive networking (Possamaï, 2000, 370).

Manuel Castells has described how networked social movements, rhizomatic, unplanned and undirected, have been an important driver of social change in the twenty-first century (Castells, 2012, 17). These movements spread like a plant rhizome, producing offshoots of new growth, each of which could independently survive and develop if isolated from the main body (Castells, 2012, 140–5, 147 and 224). For Castells these movements are increasingly significant, as much for their structure and mode of organization as for their stated aims. Their comparatively leaderless structure is both a result of and an enabler of their internal culture of radical personal autonomy (Castells, 2012, 224–34). Castells argues that this societal trend is rooted in the shift to postmodernity, but with the addition of an extra dimension of cooperation and creativity (Castells, 2000, 448–59).

The following three examples show how some authors have applied similar ideas specifically to individualized religious contexts. First, Dominic Corrywright cites Fritjof Capra's notion of the 'web of life' to suggest a paradigm shift in society from hierarchies to networks (Corrywright, 2003, 85). He cites various authors to envisage New Age spiritualities as multiple overlapping and non-hierarchical institutions and practices, such that individuals' psyches are best approached through application of the concept of a web of relationships to create socially embedded 'thick descriptions' (Corrywright, 2003, 80–96). Corrywright thus argues that these networks are informally developed and disseminated, and holistic in nature, with a close relationship existing between individuals and the shifting networks in which they participate (Corrywright, 2003, 86–8).

Second, Susan Willhauck and Jaqulyn Thorpe, arguing emically from a Methodist context, identify and advocate the emergence of a 'web style of leadership' (Willhauck and Thorpe, 2001). This constitutes a perhaps slightly self-conscious combination of the kinds of structures discussed by Corrywright with the continuation of leadership in a church context. The structure they advocate is networked and non-hierarchical, with leadership increasingly shared, and is intended to create a sense of spiritual unity while recognizing and utilizing the autonomy of individual members (Willhauck and Thorpe, 2001, 73). The structure they envisage is bounded, but firmly embedded in local and wider social networks (Willhauck and Thorpe, 2001, 150–1). It transmits itself not through the teaching of a body of knowledge but through a shared 'community of mutual learning' (Willhauck and Thorpe, 2001, 107–8).

Third, Jorg Rieger and Kwok Pui-lan discuss how the Occupy movement (a primary exemplar of the kind of movement discussed by Castells) has brought people together from a wide variety of religious traditions and contexts, and encouraged them to rethink how they organize and associate (Rieger and Kwok, 2013, 49–55). Often these interactions centred on the creation of physical spaces where individuals could come together and interact (Rieger and Kwok, 2013, 49). Rieger and Kwok use these experiences to argue for a non-hierarchical kind of religious movement with no central command, which (at least in principle) 'values the agency and self-organizing power of the people' (Rieger and Kwok, 2013, 120–1).

The contexts discussed by Corrywright, Willhauck and Thorpe and Rieger and Kwok each approximate to Castells' understanding of networked social movements to varying degrees. While Corrywright's example concerns individuals likely acting outside of formal structures, that of Willhauck and Thorpe concerns networks created within and across the boundaries of a pre-existing formal structure. Rieger and Kwok discuss networks being created between individuals who are also participating in unrelated formal religious structures. Of course, the extent to which these examples are truly individualized and truly networked, and the ways these networks realize themselves, develop and sustain themselves over time will vary, and are open to empirical investigation.

Vernacular religion is a concept that emphasizes the power of individuals to create and re-create their own religion in a 'continuous act of individual reinterpretation and negotiation of any number of influential sources' (Primiano, 2012, 383–6), and thus provides a route to contextualized study of how individualized practitioners live, interpret and express their religion. Belief is understood not as assent to closed doctrinal frameworks, but in terms of its day-to-day expression by individuals, in their discourse, their actions, and their relationships with others and with the material world (Bowman and Valk, 2012, 5–10). Individuals' religious identities are seen as multiple, shifting and often negotiated through their cultural expressions of belief (Bowman and Valk, 2012, 16). The vernacular religion approach provides a way of understanding religious belief on a purely personal level through individuals' own actions and narrative performances, using a range of methodological approaches (Primiano, 2012,

388–90) that avoid connotations of disembeddedness. It also aids understanding of religious change by charting processes of negotiation at an individual level (see, for example, Rowbottom, 2012, 99). Perhaps most importantly, vernacular religion problematizes the distinction between postmodern forms of religion and traditional institutional forms. For example, Robert Orsi's account of belief and practice within Roman Catholicism presents a picture that is very much rooted within the Catholic Church, but also surprisingly postmodern in character. It shows how Catholicism is not just a matter of top-down authority, but also a day-to-day lived expression of faith, and a dynamic and ongoing negotiation between these two (Orsi, 2005). This appears strikingly similar to the negotiation occurring between New Age spiritualities and mainstream culture (both secular and Christian) in Ingvild Saelid Gilhus' examination of public discussions of angels in Norway (Gilhus, 2012, 242).

Transmission

Gift economies, social networks and vernacular religion all give valuable insight into how individualized religion can accommodate mutualized practice through cooperation, shared leadership and negotiation. However, the notion of practice communities goes further in providing a plausible means for specifically individualized religion to accommodate the transmission of religious ideas. To properly explain how this works, it is necessary to first outline the basics of learning theory.

Traditional approaches to education were based on objectivist theories of learning, which assume that there is a single objective reality that can be correctly modelled and interpreted. In this kind of model, human thought is seen as ultimately a way of objectively representing this reality, which is independent of and external to the human mind (Vrasidas, 2000). Teaching is simply a matter of representing this external reality using theoretical models and abstract symbols, mapping this representation onto the learner's mind (Vrasidas, 2000), thereby eliciting a correct behavioural response from the learner (Leidner and Jarvenpaa, 1995, 266). The teacher is thus seen as simply a provider of pre-existing objective knowledge (Leidner and Jarvenpaa, 1995, 266).

Robert Orsi's account of religious education in the Roman Catholic Church in the mid-twentieth century illustrates how religious education can be modelled along objectivist principles (Orsi, 2005, 73–109). The process of 'formation' that he describes includes not only strictly applied instruction of what were understood as correct belief and values but also inculcation of what were understood as correct behavioural and sensory responses (Orsi, 2005, 76–7).

The Communities of Practice model, by contrast, is descended from the work of Lev Vygotsky, who understood learning not as a simple process of acquisition of knowledge and correct behaviour but as something ongoing and integral to our cultural and psychological development (Vygotsky, 1978, 84 and 90–1). Etienne Wenger, the model's major contemporary proponent, defines Communities of Practice as 'groups of people who share a concern or a passion for something they do and learn how to do it better as they interact regularly' (Wenger-Trayner and Wenger-Trayner, 2015, 1). He argues that such groups are endemic to our existence, and that the theory can be applied to any such group, however, informally constituted (Wenger, 1998, 6–7).

A Community of Practice is a community of mutual engagement, whose actions are the subject of negotiation among its members (Wenger, 1998, 73–4). This negotiation is also a negotiation of meaning, which is enhanced by the diverse perspectives and understandings of members, and leads not to them having the same views, but to a dynamically evolving negotiated shared practice (Wenger, 1998, 75–7 and 82). A Community of Practice is thus a joint enterprise, where members negotiate ongoing 'relations of mutual accountability' towards one another and the community as a whole (Wenger, 1998, 81–2). A Community of Practice will also develop for itself and then utilize a shared repertoire of resources, which facilitates engagement and practice (Wenger, 1998, 82–3). These include 'routines, words, tools, ways of doing things, stories, gestures, symbols, genres, actions, or concepts that the community has produced or adopted in the course of its existence, and which have become part of its practice', and they provide a shared sense of history and identity (Wenger, 1998, 83).

In short, a Community of Practice is a mutually engaged learning community. It provides its members with access to the competence and understanding it has generated, but also depends on their individual experience and views for the exploration and creation of new insights (e.g. see Wenger, 1998, 214). It therefore provides a shared identity of participation, predicated on the ongoing transformation of knowledge (Wenger, 1998, 215).

The elements of the Communities of Practice model provide a plausible model for transmission of ideas, beliefs and practices in an individualized setting, since they allow for these to be mutually developed, negotiated and shared while maintaining the conditions of individualization as set out in Chapter 1. As will be seen in Chapter 6, the elements of this model do fit well with the forms of engagement among the individualized religionists in this research, and in fact do a good job of explaining transmission in this context. They provide viable routes of transmission, but in a non-hierarchical way that preserves the autonomy, diversity and variant points of view of their constituent members.

The overall model of functionally viable individualized religion described in the three preceding sections centres around the notion of the individual as an assemblage interacting within a context of peer assemblages, whose actions are subjectively experienced as meaningful and self-directed, but are nevertheless rooted in those of its peers upon it, such that it can form a multiplicity of forms of engagement that do not necessarily require structures of hierarchy and power imbalance. These can be modelled, for example, in terms of systems of mutual reciprocity, networks or practice communities. The latter is especially plausible since it provides resources for transmission of ideas, beliefs and practices.

Individualization and secularization

As stated in the previous chapter, this work does not comprise a counterargument to secularization or the secularization theory. The issues and processes around secularization are complex. As we have seen, the arguments can be at cross purposes and different authors put together varying stories about how the various processes interact. As Bruce points out (Bruce 2011, 3–4), secularization theory is presented first and foremost neither as an immutable law nor as an inevitability, but a historical explanation of well-documented events and trends. I have detailed this explanation in Chapter 1, but it is worth summarizing here too. Bruce's argument is that as frameworks invest increasing amounts of authority in the individual, they lose their ability to inspire commitment (since there is no power to force 'weaker' members to do what the movement sees as right), or to sustain ongoing consensus and consequently a shared life (there being no 'coerced consensus' from above; Bruce, 2011, 114–16). Moreover, Bruce argues, the ideological commitment to the enlightened self as arbiter of truth that characterizes individualized religion runs counter to the very idea of a unified belief and will thus result in increasing levels of eclecticism that will ultimately diminish cohesion and any impetus to evangelize (Bruce, 2011, 116–18). Thus, a structural tension exists between the interests of the individual and those of the community (Bruce and Voas, 2007, 15; Bruce, 2011, 113), which mitigates against the ability of individualized religion to inspire commitment in adherents or to effect change, and ultimately to impact on wider culture or society (Bruce, 2006, 42–4).

I tend to agree with this explanation of the effects of individualization insofar as they concern how dynamic processes of individualization have provided serious, and ultimately existential, functional challenge to hierarchical and top-down religious institutions. However, Bruce makes clear that he also sees this 'epistemic individualism' as a key reason why he expects New Age and other individualistic spiritualities to have difficulties engendering ongoing levels of commitment (Bruce 2011, 112–13). This is in effect an extension of the argument to also cover religious forms that are rooted in the individualized practice of their participants. Based on the discussions in this chapter, it is this usage that I find more problematic. This is because it implicitly accepts that effectively functioning religious association needs a top-down hierarchical model of learning, predicated on objective religious knowledge that is necessary to the continuing existence of the movement. On such a view, adherents act primarily as passive recipients of knowledge rather than as its active and dynamic co-creators. There is, therefore, for a particular religious group, a correct set of answers, such that leaders who are afforded authority and power are necessary in order to disseminate, maintain and police adherence to the right view. As I have argued, individualized religion is likely to be better modelled by applying constructivist or social constructivist theories of learning that emphasize a dynamic relationship between learning, psychological development, practice, and social interaction (per Vygotsky, 1978, 89; Wenger, 1998, 4–5). Unlike religious forms structured around claims to objectivity, these subjectivity-centred religious forms are likely to be better able to cope with the consequences of epistemic individualism because they have routes to social significance and ongoing transmission available to them that are predicated on those very consequences. Developing our understanding of these forms is therefore key to our understanding of the social significance of religion in contemporary society.

3

A community of incomers

The ethnographic research on which this book is based was focused on the loose communities and networks of individualized religionist practitioners around Hebden Bridge, a valley town in West Yorkshire, UK. This chapter sets the stage by giving an overview of the town, and of the sample of participants who conduct and develop their religious lives within this environment. The chapter begins with a brief overview of the geography and history of the town and valley. This is followed by a more extended discussion of the social history of the valley since the so-called hippy influx of the early 1970s, and of the effects of the subsequent waves of incomers on local culture. We then go on to discuss the common factors about the town and valley that motivate people to move to and stay in the area, as well as local points of social fracture. The chapter concludes with a brief overview of the social and economic statuses of my sample of research participants.

Hebden Bridge and the valley

Hebden Bridge is a former textile town, located in the Upper Calder Valley, in West Yorkshire, in northern England (Figures 1 and 2). Most of the town centre lies in the bottom of a deep T-shaped valley where the River Calder is joined by two tributaries, Hebden Water (Hebden Beck) and Golden Water. The town is surrounded on all sides by steep hills, giving an impression from the town centre of being in a vast natural amphitheatre. Hebden Bridge is the middle town of a row of three small towns lying along the Calder Valley floor, flanked by Todmorden (upstream, near to the River Calder's source, often known locally as Tod) and Mytholmroyd (downstream to the east). The village of Heptonstall, up one of the surrounding hills, was the main centre of population in the area prior to the draining of the valley floor at the start of the Industrial Revolution.

Hebden Bridge is named for the old Packhorse Bridge in the town centre, where the old Long Causeway crossed Hebden Beck on its way down the Calder Valley from Manchester to Leeds. For centuries, Hebden Bridge consisted of just this bridge, an Inn and perhaps a few houses (Thomas, 2008, 33), and much of the local population lived and worked in farmsteads on the sides of the hills.

The opening of the turnpike along the valley floor in 1761 and the Rochdale Canal in 1774 saw the start of a long period of industrial transformation and major economic expansion, culminating in the opening of the railway in 1841 (Jennings, 1992, 113–22 and 158). Water-powered spinning mills opened from the 1780s, followed by steam-powered mills in the early to mid-nineteenth century. By the second half of the nineteenth century the area had become a major centre of production of both wool and cotton spinning and weaving, and by the twentieth century Hebden Bridge was becoming well known for the manufacture of fustian cloth and clothing (Jennings, 1992, 175–6), leading to its local nicknames Fustianopolis and Trouser-Town.

The Calder Valley has a long history of religious rebelliousness, dating back at least to the seventeenth-century non-conformists (Binns, 2013, 4–5). During the nineteenth century, more than a hundred non-conformist chapels in the area provided a focus for radical political activity, including Luddites, resistance to the Poor Law, Chartism and union activity (Jennings, 1992, 142–93). The area

Figure 1 Hebden Bridge town centre seen from the hillside to the east of the town.

Figure 2 St George's Square, in the centre of Hebden Bridge. The picture shows how the sides of the Calder Valley all around the town give it a feeling of being walled in. Note how the centre of the town is in shadow even though the hills above are in bright sunlight. The valley floor in which the town centre sits is navigated not just by the River Calder, but also by the Rochdale Canal, the Manchester to Leeds railway, and the A646. Todmorden and Mytholmroyd lie up and down the river valley. Heptonstall sits on the top of one of the surrounding hills, to the west.

is known for the development of workers' cooperatives and benevolent societies (Binns, 2013, 49–52, 81), most notably at Nutclough Mill.[1] In the early twentieth century, Hebden Bridge and the wider West Riding of Yorkshire became a significant centre of suffragette activity (Liddington, 2006, 81, 107–9).

The industrial era lasted until the 1960s when the collapse of the local textile industry led to the exodus of many young people in search of employment elsewhere, and a period of local economic decline (Barker, 2012a, 26–7). This period was followed in the 1970s by a countercultural influx of 'artists, writers, photographers, musicians, alternative practitioners, green and New Age activists' (Barker, 2012a, 71–2; HBW, 2016). As a result, much literature about Hebden Bridge today affords it a reputation for individualism and quirkiness, and as a centre for green and New Age activism. There is a tendency towards nicknames that highlight local nonconformity, such as 'the fourth funkiest place in the world' (HBW, 2005; Barker, 2012b), the 'lesbian capital of the UK' (Myers,

[1] See https://1nutclough.wordpress.com/history-2/

2013; Barker, 2012b), and less positively 'a hippie idyll scarred by heroin' (Myers, 2013). However, while there has been some socio-geographic study of the town (see Morris and Cant, 2006), the contemporary religious character of the area remains significantly under-researched.

Natives and incomers

Writers about the history of Hebden Bridge (e.g. see Barker, 2012a, 72) and also local residents (HBLHS, 2017) tend to see the so-called hippy influx as a defining event in the history of the town and the valley. The term refers to the arrival in the early to mid-1970s of a significant number of students, squatters and counterculturals to what was then a rundown and increasingly derelict mill town.

Steve's family was from the valley, and he himself was brought up in neighbouring Halifax. He remembers the valley towns before the influx as self-contained, hardy and tight-knit communities with a keen sense of mutual rivalry:

> I went to Calder High School for a year. I remember being told: 'you make sure you get on the right bus, otherwise you'll get beaten up'. It was a very strong rivalry between the different communities, and it came out in the kids more than anything else. It's not that long since there was gangs of kids in Hebden, smashing cars, and similarly [in] Mytholmroyd all the cars were getting keyed by a gang of kids from Hebden. Not that long since. . . . I've not felt personally threatened very often. But then you don't show fear. If you show fear you become a victim. But yeah, I have an old book about Halifax. Written about 1800. And I remember it quotes a letter from somebody, who said: 'the inhabitants of this town are as rough and as wild as the surrounding terrain'. And I think there's truth in that. . . . I just think you have to be vigorous to survive.

Steve also talks of a historical lack of respect for authority among valley locals:

> That was the other thing about this area, was the gentry were not the richest people about. So there was never that much respect for the Tory thing. Because the gentry weren't – you know, didn't carry all the prestige and all the rest of it. It was never true round here. I mean this part of West Yorkshire – the Valley, Halifax, what not. They were, yeah. . . . There was not that respect [for hierarchy]. . . . I've worked as a fruit picker, you know, in all sorts of rural areas, and been astonished at the sort of forelock-tugging sort of way people are in the countryside. . . .

So maybe it's part of our person of Yorkshiremen – Yorkshire persons – is that blunt speaking, of basically the lack of unearned respect.

Jess, who also grew up in the valley, talks about the feel of Hebden Bridge in the 1960s and how it has changed since then:

> You know, my life was school, and then at the weekend I'd be shoved in the Working Men's Club back room, with cockles and crisps, while my Mum and Dad did their bingo and ballroom dancing. . . . Somehow Hebden had its really dark times, and the black satanic mills and the children working here and all that. And it feels like it's changing, because it's gone through that depth of real darkness. And I mean you used to just drive in here and all the buildings were black – absolutely black with all the soot from the mills and everything. It was a very dark place.

Steve recalls how he, as a local, became involved in the lifestyle of the new arrivals:

> I remember hearing about these hippies who'd bought the houses at Foster Clough. And these were my people really. But I didn't know anybody round here really, because I'd been at boarding school for ten years. But the summer of love was when I was 15, and that permeated everything. The sort of ideas that came out of that. '67, if you like. I mean I'd been to college. Done all that. Hippy was a sort of a style, but there was a whole ideal behind it about alternative culture. And anyway, an old girlfriend of mine came back from university and I knew her from Halifax. She came to live in Mytholmroyd. I got invited up there about '73. And suddenly I was with people who were like me. And never looked back from that point onwards actually. . . . Always, within the alternative kind of world, there was all these ideas that involved Yoga and Buddhism and all the rest of it, as well as all the acid. And drugs in general to be honest. It was a sort of an enlightening thing rather than something you just did for pure indulgence [laughs]. And Hebden at that point had lost half of its population since 1945, as had Todmorden and most of the places through the valley. They demolished a lot of houses. All underdwellings were declared unfit for human habitation, and were in fact empty.[2] Nearly all of them. So there was loads of places to squat. And houses were cheap to buy anyway. And that is what brought lots of people in. . . . They used to come in groups almost, from different universities. And they were mostly graduates at that point, the early seventies. . . . And a community just was created really, within a couple of years. It was quite extraordinary. This is like hundreds. It wasn't just Hebden you know. It was Todmorden. It was the whole Upper Valley.

---

[2] Underdwellings are a kind of housing particular to Hebden Bridge, in which one row of terraced houses is built directly on top of another to make efficient use of space on the steep hillsides of the valley. See Figure 3.

Figure 3 A terrace of underdwellings in Hebden Bridge, seen from above and below. This kind of housing comprises one terrace of houses built directly on top of another. The top row is accessed by a road higher up the hill than the road from which the lower terrace is accessed. The lower terrace is in effect built into the hill. Testimony from research participants suggests that in the 1970s whole rows of these houses were abandoned and then served as sites for squatters and communities of students, who gave them a new lease of life. While some were demolished, those that remain are now a popular form of housing in the area.

One of the early incomers was Xia, a former student who was heavily involved with the Manchester hippy scene before moving to the valley in 1971:

> We spent all our time [in Manchester] and created lots of networks, and we wanted to move out into the country. Because part and parcel of that living an alternative lifestyle was to try to be a bit more self-sufficient. We were a bit more idealistic. So we were looking for somewhere in the country, and we found this quite derelict farmhouse through some friends that had also moved out here from Manchester. . . . The house was very, very cheap. I mean it was less than two grand [laughs], to buy a farmhouse and barn at that time. And it was derelict, but you could get grants in those days. . . . But very quickly we learned that there were other people who had moved into Foster Clough at Heights Road. There was a group of terraces there that some students from Bradford had bought. So there was a little group of people there, there was us at our farmhouse. . . . And there was another little settlement of people that again had come from Leeds or Bradford University. So we all knew each other and we were all very different from the existing indigenous population. The young people had all left. The industry had died.

Kate arrived in 1975, by which time the community of incomers was established:

> I'd had enough of squatting in London. It was – it was difficult and stressful and I was looking for something new. And I came here and I loved the area and the land so much. And I had some friends here. And I thought why go back? Why go back to London was the question, and I thought – yeah why? Why would I? So I went to get the cat and the rucksack. Life was a lot simpler then. I didn't have many possessions. So I've lived here since 1975. So I was part of the first wave of hippie culture here. Which was great. And it was a very special time. And many of us were looking for new ways of living, which involved spirituality and food. I was in a food co-op. And we were exploring Yoga and meditation. . . . I've got special links with those people from that time. They're like family. They're my tribe.

Of my twenty-nine study participants, eight were present at the time of the hippy influx (six incomers and two natives). As exemplified by these accounts, they speak of a ready availability of cheap or derelict housing (including whole rows of abandoned houses ripe for squatting), which enabled groups of graduates and university students to squat en masse and create their own communities. Those young people are described by their older selves as having been strongly idealistic. They wanted to pioneer new ways of living and new forms of community, with the express intention of changing society for the better. They tended to link this with 'hippy ideals' of love and peace, with an anti-authoritarian or even explicitly anarchistic left political outlook, and with environmentalism and/or gender politics:

> You recognized each other instantly. That's what makes community. And we were very kind with each other. You know. This was alternative society, you know. (Steve)

> We definitely wanted to live a certain way. . . . I think it was the 'love and peace, man'. You know. And all that stuff. It was just the classic – you know. But we really felt that at that time. (Wendy)

> The people that came in, they had to build communities. They had no neighbourhood of their own. They had no family. Friends they could build up. So the avenues through which connections were built were different. For local people it was the Labour Party. For other people it was music. For some people who lived near the tops,[3] it was trying to find new ways of living on the land. And for others of us it was just the general environmental, and I think broadly spiritual outlook that pervaded many of us. . . . And many of us were political. But also had this sense of kinship with land. (Andy)

Although a couple now express mild embarrassment at the naivety of their former selves, none admits to having moved significantly away from those ideals. Some also went on to connect their youthful (and in some cases more recent) expression of these politics with the use of mind-expanding and hallucinogenic drugs such as LSD and magic mushrooms, and some with spiritual experimentation, for example, through yoga, meditation or interest in Paganism or Eastern religions, many having been on trips to India during the 1970s or 1980s.

A minority of influx incomers (known locally as Premis) became involved with the Divine Light Mission, a spiritual group centred around an Indian guru known as Prem Rawat.[4] However Premis remained integrated in the wider alternative culture of the area, as illustrated by these two quotes, from a Premi and a non-Premi:

> A number of people did not like Divine Light Mission as it was called then – didn't like it at all. And if you brought it up it was like 'Oh shut up!'. They didn't want to know. You know, a lot of people didn't want to know about it at all. Some did, some didn't. But I think we were all striving the same way, if you know what I mean. We all had the same principles at the core of us really, I think. Be kind to each other, and respect each other, and you know all those sort of things. That was still there, whoever you were. That seemed to be a general – and a lot of our friends weren't involved with it at all.

---

[3] 'Tops' is a local term for the hills of the South Pennines around the Upper Calder Valley.
[4] See https://www.premrawat.com

There was quite a lot of our friends into Divine Light, and that – quite a lot of people. I never quite understood how they – it seems to be something they were caught up in and I never quite understood what it was. But they did remain good friends.

The sense here seems to have been that the community, friendships and generic hippy ideals were more fundamental to both sides than whether or not they subscribed to a particular belief or group.

Another important aspect of the original hippy scene seems to have been music. As Wendy puts it,

We did used to come together due to music. . . . The big building where Oasis News is used to be a ballroom upstairs. And so bands would play in there and at the Trades Club. . . . I think we were around at a really fortunate time when music was really good, you know. . . . It was creative as well, but I think if you – say if you're a musician or an artist or a dancer or whatever, I think you – sort of the concentration of what you're doing, you hit a certain point in yourself where you forget everything and you're just being, aren't you, you're just in the flow.

Because these young hippies tended to be university graduates and therefore educated and middle class, they would have been culturally very different to the older, less well educated and more working-class valley natives with whom they came in contact. It is perhaps surprising, therefore, that accounts from natives and incomers suggest the two groups got on fairly well. Jess puts this down to tolerance of the locals, which she ascribes to the enclosed nature of the valley:

It's always been a very tolerant place, way back when. Because you know it was like, the hippies came in the seventies and sort of squatted a load of houses and stuff. And you had the farm people, and the mill workers, which my parents were. But because you're in this little space, it's like you have to learn to tolerate people, because you're in the little space. But there's always been, you know, a massive tolerance here. There always has been.

Another factor suggested by Andy was a hard-headed awareness on the part of the locals that, many native young people having moved away in search of employment, the alternative to the presence of the hippies would be worse:

I'm always mindful of what somebody said to me, a local person said to me in the 1970s. I was wearing waist length hair and a beard sort of down to my chest, and he said 'Eh, you're funny looking buggers, but we're bloody glad you're coming to stay here to live!', and meaning it wasn't becoming a second home nexus, which it could have been, very easily, because of the dales and so on. So it could have been depopulated by the young and then depopulated by part-timers. Because of the hippy influx, it kept the shops open. Yeah. . . . So the community, I'm pretty sure, was grateful for that.

A third factor is suggested by the commonly told story of the 'yellow hippies', a group of reputedly jaundiced (hence the adjective 'yellow') out-of-town travellers that passed through, inadvertently showing the settled hippies in a good light by comparison. This version of the story is also by Andy:

> There was a time in the seventies when the hippy communes, the hippy traveller people came through and camped out somewhere and then the crime rate seemed to shoot up a little bit – a lot of petty theft, shoplifting and so on. And again, famously, one lady was famously quoted in the local paper saying 'They're not like our hippies!' And at that point, that's when I think we began to be accepted! [laughs] There are 'ippies and there are 'ippies. There's one lot up in the teepees, and there's ones that live next door to us, who seem quite nice.

Since the initial influx of the 1970s, there appears to have been pretty much continuous immigration into the area. Over time, at least in Hebden Bridge, incomers seem to have largely (but not wholly) replaced the former population, and the immigration to the valley appears to have fuelled an ongoing evolution of local culture. My research participants divide roughly into three groups: those who were present during the hippy influx of the 1970s (eight participants); those who arrived in the 1980s and 1990s (nine participants); and those who have arrived since the millennium (eleven participants). Though somewhat arbitrary and with very fuzzy boundaries, this division is useful in helping understand how local culture has developed.

The members of the 1970s hippy influx who still live in the valley tend to see themselves as a kind of ongoing nucleus. Many still meet socially on a monthly basis (one person told me the generally accepted criterion for membership of this group is having arrived before 1980). As suggested earlier, the story that underpins this group's modern-day view of itself is one of the hippy influx having created a new kind of post-industrial culture based on a new set of ideals, but in relative harmony with both the native townsfolk and their pre-existing culture of hard-nosed but tolerant community.

The middle group arrived after the alternative culture had already become established. Typically, their introduction to the valley and its alternative culture was first-hand – for example, through somebody who already lived there. Tara, for example, needed to move out of a house in Bradford at short notice:

> [Our Landlord's friend] lived just outside of Hebden Bridge, so she said that we could stay at hers for a bit until we decided what to do. So we ended up staying

at hers. She'd just opened a shop in Hebden Bridge selling things she imported from Africa. And my husband at the time was from Kenya. And she was really tired and needed a break. So we ended up living in her house and running her little African shop in Hebden Bridge, with my African husband. And it was just like – it just was perfect. We fell on our feet.

Some of the arrivals from this time came from other parts of Lancashire or Yorkshire, attracted by the local countryside, and only became aware of the alternative scene after they arrived. Sometimes, as was the case for Fran, this was years later.

> I've lived in Hebden Bridge for roundabout 35 years. I did not know about Hebden Bridge before we moved here. I lived in St. Helens before then. Flat. And we moved to buy a beautiful farm with my sister and her husband. And we didn't realise what an alternative, rich community it was, until we'd settled here. I worked full time for ten years whilst we were here, and didn't have much link with Hebden Bridge. But then when I took early retirement I began to realise how rich it was.

By the 1980s increasing numbers of lesbians were moving to the area around Todmorden and Hebden Bridge, as it became increasingly known as a safe space to be out. While some of my participants did talk about having been involved in a 'dyke scene', or having once had separatist views, over the years lesbian circles seem to have become increasingly integrated into wider Hebden culture.

While the hippy influx clearly did mark a turning point both in the economic fortunes of the area and in local culture, arguably just as big a turning point happened (roughly speaking) around the turn of the century when the area started to become perceived externally as a desirable place to live. Tourism (focusing on both the countryside and the projection of unique culture) has become an increasingly important part of the economy, and the gentrification of the area that was already occurring seems to have gathered pace. Victor, who moved to Hebden Bridge in the 1990s, describes how the character of the town as he sees it has changed since then:

> I kind of first came to Hebden Bridge in 1988. And I wasn't living here then, but I was coming here regularly. So like many people you start coming to Hebden Bridge at some point. But I decided to make the move. I'm not part of the – there's a more modern trend. I came round about 1999 I think. There was a very different town then. So most of what you see out there was not here. In fact where we're sitting in now was a school uniform shop. And it had this set of plastic mannequins, that had a strange eroticism about them. It was very

odd. It was very Royston Vasey. And there was a hippy shop called Lancaster House, which was very small. Nothing big like Earth Spirit. No Yoga Centre or anything like that, really. The Hope Centre wasn't there. All the things we think are that side of Hebden Bridge didn't exist at that point. But there were meetings. Groups of people meeting. There was – so we're only talking like twenty years ago. Obviously there was a lot of alternative lifestyles here, you know.

Victor's account suggests a culture that has grown increasingly commodified, as commercial outlets have opened that cater to an alternative, New Age and spirituality-related market (Figure 4). Arguably, the hippy influx itself has now been appropriated as a kind of founding myth for Hebden Bridge's twenty-first-century media/marketing branding as the 'fourth funkiest town in the world' and the 'Glastonbury of the North' (HBW, 2005; CoolPlaces, 2015). This brasher, more extrovert and commercial side to Hebden Bridge has not supplanted the

Figure 4 Leaflets and posters on a window in central Hebden Bridge. Spiritual groups and practices jostle for attention with concerns ranging from music to environmental and humanitarian aid.

culture that was there before the millennium, and it has brought economic growth to the area, but there is a sense that it is unwelcome to many. A number of my participants expressed disquiet about the ways in which Hebden Bridge has evolved in recent years, as exemplified by this quote from Emma:

> I still struggle with Hebden, because it's changed so much. It was very rough and ready. Everybody was poor. People living in squats. . . . But it was – life was simple and we were really welcomed, even though we were offcumdens, which was an important part of it. . . . But now Hebden has become such a prosperous little bubble that it's alienated from the rest of the valley, which I think is really sad. . . . Since Radio 4 and the Guardian got hold of Hebden it's lost a lot of its spirit. It's lost its wildness. It's lost its spontaneity. . . . They're all terribly gentrified, middle class. It's not – Tod is more authentic. To me, it's more like Lancashire. It's more like the little industrial towns that scrape by, rather than the flash opulence that we have here.[5]

As Emma suggests, Hebden Bridge has become the centre of the local tourist industry, and has become more prosperous and more widely known than the surrounding population centres. These, together with its picturesqueness, have led to Hebden Bridge acquiring a local reputation for (in the exact words of more than one participant) being 'up itself'. That is, as having become somewhat twee, pretentious and self-important, while at the same time having an air of fakeness about it. Among my participants it is often negatively compared with Todmorden, which is seen as being more down to earth and as more in touch with its Northern roots.

Eleven of my twenty-nine participants arrived in the valley after the millennium. While it is still common for them to have known someone who lived here before coming, prior awareness of the town's alternative reputation seems to be a bigger factor in their decision to move to the valley. Zena is a good example:

> We lived in Manchester for a while and had our first child. And so it became unsuitable for us to live in Manchester any more. . . . So we were looking for a child-friendly place, and my husband has a friend here who is a film director. . . . So we visited first. So we came to see our friend. And also we heard about Incredible Edible, and just all the sort of unique cultural things that are going on here. So we moved about eight years ago. . . . Since then I've developed

---

[5] 'Offcumden' or 'offcumdens' is a local term for incomers to the area. 'Tod' is a commonly used local colloquialism for the town of Todmorden.

lots of links, in Todmorden and Hebden Bridge, within all sorts of communities – religious, artistic, whatever.

As discussed later on in this chapter, a number of both recent and earlier incomers to the area identify the existence of some forms of alternative spiritual activity that they see as narcissistic and/or commodified, and which they actively seek to distance themselves from. Victor provides a good example of this:

> Selling, selling, you know, spiritual garbage to tourists mostly. Fake spiritual garbage to tourists. You can't tell what's real and what's not real.

One factor behind this kind of attitude could be an attempt to draw distinction between this and one's own spiritual activity as a way of supporting one's own claims to authenticity and depth. However, it is also of note that the distinction being made coheres fairly well with the theoretical distinction highlighted in Chapter 2 between disembedded and embedded forms of individualization. Such arguments among participants could then merely represent attempts to draw this kind of theoretical distinction.

So why here?

Although all but two of my interviewees are incomers, most of them have lived in the valley for decades – some for not far short of fifty years. For these people, the questions of what attracted them to the valley and what has made them stay for so long are not only closely related but often difficult to tease apart. This section, then, looks at what it is about the valley and the town(s) that people claim has attracted them to the area and motivated them to stay, and also what (if anything) they think is special or unique about the area.

In answering this question, the countryside and the sense of community were both mentioned pretty universally. As these three quotes illustrate, the countryside tended to feature in terms of its natural beauty (Figure 5), its variety, its accessibility or its suitability for walking:

> I was attracted by the stunning countryside. I've always wanted to live in the countryside and as soon as I went up on the tops – it's just a hidden gem. (Yvonne)

> I like the beautifulness of the countryside, and being able to have access to shops and everything and the railway, and good road connections and everything, but also live in the woods basically. My house is in the woods and it's very nice. (Ros)

> Well actually I'd been coming here for forty years as a fell walker. (Irene)

Figure 5 The Upper Calder Valley, looking over Hebden Bridge from the road to Heptonstall. The beauty of the countryside and its opportunities for hiking are quoted by participants as significant attractors to the valley. Some claim particular spiritual connection with the area.

The sense of community in the valley tended to be associated in answers with an atmosphere of tolerance and openness, and/or with the anti-authoritarian and communitarian political history of the valley:

> Rich diversity of people. Friendliness. Sense of community. Meeting the same people in the streets. Lovely shopkeepers. Familiarity with diverse people from different strands of life, making it feel comfortable. (Fran)

> A very strong sense of community I've found here . . . but a sense that your ideas resonate here rather than you being considered a kind of complete oddball. (Becks)

> This community is vital to me. Hebden Bridge is vital. It gives me the emotional underpinning. . . . One of the things I was drawn to here was because it was a centre for the Co-operative Movement, in the 1870s. And setting up this wonderful textile co-operative at Nutclough Mills. That influenced me a lot. I wanted to be somewhere where people working together, drawing together, mattered hugely. (Carey)

This idea of the valley as a place of creativity is an important one to a number of people, who commonly tend to cite the presence of a large and active community of musicians, artists, literary folk or activists:

> There's so many artists [and] musicians here. You know, and I didn't know anything about that, and I thought, you know, because I'm an artist myself and it's strange. I just think it has this draw for creative people. (Yvonne)

A third factor was a tendency among some participants to describe themselves as having or feeling some kind of spiritual connection with the town and valley, sometimes using it as a way of bringing the countryside and community together into one answer:

> We didn't move for spiritual reasons per se. We moved for our children to have, you know, like green safe environment, from Manchester City Centre. But I feel, especially the countryside here is intensely spiritual. Intensely. I mean it just shines through. . . . You can feel it at the tops. (Zena)

> I felt a great sense of – in a Shamanic – a deep sense of connection with aspects of nature, of the land here and its residents. I've found that [to be] a great part of the sense of belonging, and the sense of nurturance that I've experienced here. (Liam)

A few go further, explicitly or implicitly ascribing a kind of agency to the valley and town, such that it has power to draw people in, support and nurture them, and on occasion eject them again.

> I don't know, there's just something about the place that draws you to it. . . . Yeah I was just drawn in. . . . And of course when you're up – out there, you do feel spiritual, because you know you drop everything and you're walking along and you just – it speaks to you, the countryside. (Yvonne)

Sometimes participants linked spiritual significance to the geology of the area:

> There's a lot of knowledge about healing dynamics in Hebden Bridge. I think it's a powerful spot because three rivers meet here, and for a lot of us the water of life is a very connecting flow. And we can sort of use the imagery of that to sort of send out healing as well as try to heal. (Diane)

> My friend said Hebden Bridge is like a crystal ball. We've got the hill on the south, Fairfield. We've got the Old Town hill and Heptonstall hill. And we're like on this T-valley junction, with three hills around. What is inside the hills? She said it's quartz. And quartz is like crystal. She said there's like a crystal ball. And we are like in a pressure cooker. This crystal ball is resonating and vibrating with us and inspiring us and amplifying our energies. That's her theory. So that may

be the landscape. But also my experience is that if the landscape is flat it's quite likely it inspires the spirit and your mental horizon also is flat. And when there is a big dynamic landscape, somehow it makes you more deep in the soul maybe, or rise the spirit more up. (Hugo)

The form and extent of connection with the local landscape varied hugely, such that it might be possible to conceive of a spectrum of views. On one end of the spectrum lie some of those who identify themselves as having Pagan, Shaman or New Age views, who tend to be more likely to ascribe supernatural, mystical or magical links to it, and are more likely to personify the local environment:

When we came here it was raining. . . . And they expected another flood. . . . And it was very strange, real feeling. And so this woman said, 'You know what? That force which brought you to Hebden Bridge will look after you.' And I call it maybe the spirit of Hebden Bridge. And I feel like there's something. You know, this, the spirit is very strong. (Hugo)

At the other end lie the few who explicitly deny any kind of spiritual connection with the land or with local history. In the middle would then lie those who talk of connection – even spiritual or religious connection – with the local landscape, but do so in a more material or physical way.

The landscape puts walls on your vision. . . . Some people couldn't bear it, and decamped. You're used to it in 18 months. If you're still here after 18 months you're beginning to make it home. We used to say, the saying used to be, whether the valley accepts you, or rejects you. I think it's the other way around, really. But it does indicate that there's a communication. There's a dialogue between the valley and the people who live in it. If you're a valley type, you'll stay. If you're not a valley type then you'll cut your losses. You'll get out. (Andy)

Unsurprisingly, those who talk less about spiritual connection with the local landscape (or deny it completely) tend to be among those who claim a Humanist, Quaker or Buddhist orientation, and their practices tend to be less closely connected with elements of the land.

Social pressures

Hebden Bridge and the wider valley today are a curious mix of the ethereal and the practical, the parochial and the metropolitan, the affluent and the socially disadvantaged. While there is increasing affluence across the valley, there are also significant social pressures. It is perhaps interesting that a number of my participants speak of the valley as having 'darkness' or a 'dark side', and/or as having had times of darkness in the past. This section looks at three areas of social pressure that are particularly relevant with respect to the participants in this research.

One of the points of social pressure is generational. The majority of my research sample is of the generation who were in their twenties at the time of the 1970s hippy influx. As discussed earlier, these people have a similar outlook, and a particular set of assumptions, politics and cultural views. Their sense of community could well, in part, be facilitated by this uniformity. This generation brought with them very liberal social views and (among other things) a positive attitude to drugs. It has been claimed that this has led to a significant drug problem among the children of this generation in both Hebden Bridge and Todmorden (e.g. see Myers, 2013), and indeed a number of my interviewees knew of people in the next generation who had become addicted to drugs. In addition, interviewee data suggested that a laissez-faire attitude to discipline as parents among the influx generation has led to a problem with antisocial behaviour among the young, and that increasing pressure on house prices and the relative lack of well-paid local employment has placed particular economic pressures on the young. Fran describes the pressures on the younger generation:

> But I also think there's heroin addiction, and drinking, and there's a culture that's an underbelly, as was shown in Happy Valley.[6] So I do think there's a dark side, and we have to be aware of that all the time. In the park there are quite a lot of people that are users, and there can be an antisocial element. And at festivals for example the traditional fireworks on the park had to be cancelled because there was a lot of antisocial behaviour. So there could be a dark youth culture. Some of my nephews and nieces have had to get out of Hebden Bridge because they couldn't get away from the drinking and the smoking culture. . . . There are quite a lot of suicides happening in Hebden Bridge area, especially in young people. It might be to do with the economic situation generally. So I can't put my finger on what it is. . . . It could be that it's a new culture. And I think that a lot of parents have been very laissez-faire.

A second point of pressure is the high level of economic and social inequality in the valley. While some of my participants were relatively well-paid professionals or retired professionals, others were surviving on very low incomes. In some

---

[6] *Happy Valley* was a somewhat gritty 2014 BBC television crime drama set in contemporary Hebden Bridge and the surrounding valley.

cases this was through a deliberate lifestyle choice, but not in all cases. While there does seem to be a fairly vibrant internal economy, whereby the more wealthy professionals bring money into the valley that then circulates round through a kind of odd-job culture, there are a large number of people who have lived outside of formal employment for many years and who would find it very difficult to move back into that world. These difficulties are reinforced by government benefit policies that are increasingly punitive. Community-run initiatives such as the Real Junk Food Project (Figure 6), attempt to fill the gap. One of my participants describes the difficulty that exists for those on low income in the valley:

> I think we need a food bank in the middle valley. Because people are still getting sanctioned. People are still on very low incomes. You can't walk to Todmorden or Halifax and walk back with food. And the bus fare may be too expensive. It could be a fiver, four pounds fifty each way – no not each way but for the day. That's too much out of a small budget or no budget. So I have a dream of not just a food bank, but many of the things that Quaker Social Action are doing in the East End, around debt counselling, funeral plans, counselling, all kinds of things.

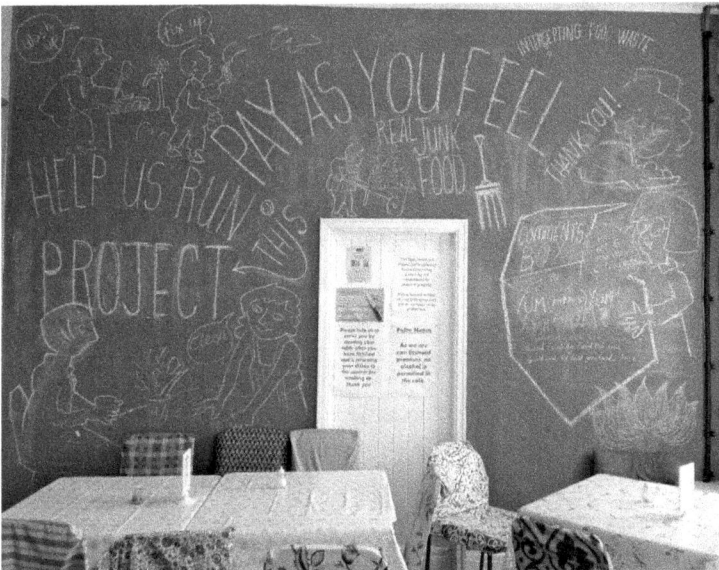

Figure 6 The Real Junk Food Project, a café in the middle of Hebden Bridge, positions itself as both a social and an environmental project. Food is offered on a 'pay as you feel' basis.

These issues are further exacerbated by Hebden Bridge's self-image as something of a sanctuary for those in need of healing and support. As one participant put it,

It still feels like a very safe place. And I think that's why a lot of people come here. . . . It has a bit of a reputation as a place for wounded people. And people come here when they've been damaged. And I think one of the problems is that they do get stuck. . . . I think people come here, usually after divorces and after marriage breakdowns and things like that – relationship breakdowns, and you tend to get this kind of polarized side to things as well. But that safety aspect, I think, people need somewhere to kind of be safe. A sanctuary. And Hebden is a sanctuary. . . . [But] I think it tends to be hiding more than healing, a lot of the time. Because Hebden has a bubble effect. And so a lot of people are wounded and use that as their identity. The wounded healer archetype is very strong here. And unfortunately we're not honest about it. The town has a dishonesty about it. This sounds like I don't love Hebden Bridge. I do, but as someone grounded in Zen and Jung [laughs] I can't kind of pretend that I don't see. . . . So Hebden denies a large part of itself. It denies its wounded self, and also the gentrification of Hebden denies the existence of the working class people who are here, the drug problem that's here, both in the older Yorkshire people who are here, shall we say, and those young people too. And there's almost like a kind of hidden underclass.

The claim, which does seem borne out by my observations, is that the valley's physical characteristics, Hebden Bridge's self-image as a place of healing and the increasing gentrification of the area have together led to the existence of an underclass, formed of both incomers and natives, many of whom are functionally unemployable, poor and/or vulnerable.

A third point of social pressure relates to the environment, and is related to political activity. As a deep river valley, the Upper Calder Valley is prone to flooding, and this has not been helped by farming practices in some higher parts of the Pennines. A particularly serious flood hit Hebden Bridge on Boxing Day 2015, with devastating effects on local homes and businesses (Figure 7). One participant talked about the effects of this flood on the local community:

Even if you weren't personally flooded, I know at least three people who were flooded whose lives have just been turned upside down, and who've really just needed a lot of holding and support to re-establish themselves, get back to a home that they want to live in. Two people I know are still living in quite strange temporary accommodation that is quite difficult to live in. So I think it brought out a kind of nurturing of each other, and just trying to help in whatever way you could. It was quite interesting actually, because you could see the stark nature of what happened here in the world. Because there's this one coffee shop called

Figure 7 After-effects of the 2015 Boxing Day flood in Hebden Bridge.

Marco's. When the flooding happened, Marco's gave out free tea and coffee and pizza. They were just brilliant. There were a few other shops that actually put their prices up. One that was the only pub open, and the shop that was the only shop open took all their special offers off and stuff. And people noticed. And you think, that is really not on, doing that. And it was the more national kind of supermarket chain in Hebden that did that. But for me, and for loads of other

Figure 7 After-effects of the 2015 Boxing Day flood in Hebden Bridge (Continued).

people who noticed this, like I'm totally faithful to Marco's now. And [there were] Syrian refugees, and people from Bradford, coming with food. You know, you just get bombarded, 'Asians are terrorists', and 'they're killing us', and it just proves in one moment, in such a powerful way what a load of rubbish that is. So that was pretty amazing. It was bonding and that to me is – you know, the true nature of spirituality is that we – we're bonded, so we don't hurt each other, because we're bonded really, the way you wouldn't hurt a family member. It just changed the way you view things.

There is a general perception among my participants that although these floods were highly traumatic, the response of the town to them brought people together and ultimately had a positive effect on the local sense of community.

Given both the ongoing local danger of flooding and the recent social history of the area, it is perhaps unsurprising that there is a high level of environmental activism, including interest in promulgating the ideals of permaculture, and involvement in and support for protests against fracking that were occurring across Yorkshire and Lancashire during my fieldwork. Many of my participants and others I met have been involved in protests of one sort or another over the years, especially Peace Activism, and despite the relative wealth in the valley, both the Green Party and Labour Party are very strong.

Participants

The participants in this study were chosen primarily for their involvement in non-traditional, non-institutionalized or self-driven religious activity. About three quarters of the sample are women and about three quarters are in their sixties or above, all but one of the rest being in their forties or fifties. Over two thirds of the overall sample are university educated, with roughly half of these having gone on to study at postgraduate level. Subjects studied at university have tended to be the social sciences, humanities (especially literature) or medicine. In interviews a number of participants connected their study in social sciences with an interest in radical, left wing or anarchistic politics. While some of these came from relatively privileged backgrounds, others came from working-class backgrounds and talked of their university education as having provided them with opportunities that their parents would not have had.

The majority of participants (around two thirds) are either in retirement already or talked of being in the process of preparing to transition to retirement. A few have retired and then gone on to do other work, for example, teaching or spirituality-related activities. Only a few of the overall sample are currently in full-time employment. The rest either work part time (sometimes doing a variety of kinds of casual and paid work, usually within the valley) or are not in paid employment. A number of participants, particularly in this latter group, are involved in voluntary work of one sort or another, for example, serving in charity shops or spirituality-related activities), and the dividing lines between unemployment, casual employment and part-time employment seem difficult to draw in some of these cases. The fact that a very large proportion of participants are retired or not in full-time employment explains why they are generally able to attend regular activities that take place during weekdays.

At least half of the sample either work or have worked in caring professions (mostly in the fields of social work, care work or medicine). Of the rest, about two thirds work or have worked in creative or media-related fields, ranging from writing and scriptwriting to art, craft and music. Quite a small number of the sample earn part or all of their living directly from spirituality-related activities, and a couple of these have made a deliberate lifestyle decision to downsize from previous higher paid full-time employment to do so. Overall there is some crossover between the various types of employment undertaken, especially among those who are employed part time or casually.

While I did not ask questions that directly probed this, it is likely that a majority of the sample is relatively affluent, having incomes either from paid employment or retirement funds. However, it is certainly the case that not all participants are affluent, and it is likely that the differences in economic situation are quite pronounced. Anecdotal evidence (both from my participants and wider informal conversations) suggests the existence of a fairly robust local micro-economy, whereby those with significant incomes bring money in, which then circulates around the valley supporting a wider range of people. This micro-economy may be facilitated by the relative lack of chain stores in the area that would take money out of the system. It is tempting to speculate as to whether the growth of this local micro-economy and also the recent gentrification and commodification of Hebden Bridge are at least in part due to the increasing numbers of affluent retirees in and around the town, as the generation of the original hippy influx has come to reach retirement age.

All participants in this project perceive themselves as having a high level of personal control over the direction and character of their own spiritual lives. However, most are also involved with various groups or group activities, and many identify themselves as falling into one or more religious categories according to the character or content of their practice and belief. Moreover, many describe occasions where their religious lives have been affected by factors external to themselves, and the boundaries between their religious lives and their other activities are also extremely hard to pin down. Their religious identities are therefore best thought of as complex and unique interweavings of their own subjective perceptions, perceptions of others about them, their actions, their engagements, and their affiliations. The diversity of these patterns of religious experience and practice is such that focusing on profiling just a few individuals in detail would be unlikely to yield very generalizable data. In the next chapter, I will therefore tease out some common patterns among, and distinctions between, different individuals' religious lives. I will do this by focusing on some exemplar affiliations, practices, orientations and engagements, and highlighting the various roles these may play.

Conclusion

The sample of participants is not intended to be representative of the local population. Rather, they are chosen as connected example cases of a particular kind of religious stance and experience. They do tend to have a fairly common set of cultural reference points, and in terms of background and socio-economic status, they are not very heterogeneous. Whether they arrived in the 1970s or not, many of the individuals in this population were in their twenties during that time, and despite the diversity of religious practice, socio-economic status and personal histories, there appears to be some unifying commonality of experience among them, which links to the ideals and lifestyle of the so-called hippy influx. While there are a number of social and economic pressures in evidence, there is evidence of cohesiveness and a strong local community spirit.

While all fit the definition of individualized religionists that I set out in Chapter 1, the participants in this research have a wide variety of religious histories, interests and practices. The next chapter will go on to delve further into the religious practices of this group of people, reiterating the point that although their religious practice does tend to be individualized, it is also highly socially embedded. Chapters 5 and 6 will then go on to examine the complexities of the relationship between their status as individualized practitioners and their engagement with others.

4

A diversity of practice

The previous chapter gave an overview of the development of Hebden Bridge and the Upper Calder Valley as a case study of an active centre of individualized religion and related practice. This is a vicinity in which creativity and religious individuality meet and feed off one another (see Figure 8). Many practitioners in this community are individualized (in that they prioritize their own subjectivity and see religious authority as residing primarily with themselves as individuals), and therefore insist on the importance of their own personal control of their religious lives. However, it should already be apparent that many of these practitioners are far from being socially isolated. In fact, they illustrate how the relationship between religious individuals and their various communities can be complex, multilayered and far from consistent. This chapter approaches individualized practitioners through their practices, and therefore also through their relationships with the wider cultures and environments in which they live and through which they collaborate to build their personal and communal religious identities.

Claiming the freedom to choose

Widespread among my research participants (and also apparent in the wider community) is an attitude of openness to a wide variety of religious and religion-related stimuli. Practitioners feel justified in looking for religious ideas from whatever sources present themselves and confident in making their own evaluations as to their utility. This quote from Cathy exemplifies how participants are aware that this 'pick-and-mix' kind of approach has sometimes been dismissed by commentators, and yet embrace it nonetheless:

> [Pick-and-mix is] a bit of a cliché for New Age stuff, but I think it is what I do. And not just that, but the continuity between traditions. The mystical stuff

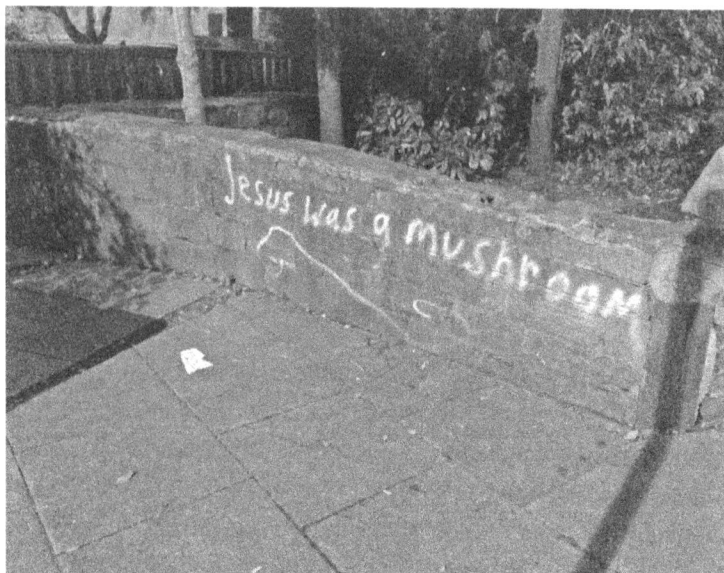

Figure 8 Graffiti found on a wall in the centre of Hebden Bridge.

tends to be much the same wherever you go. So you can pick up ideas from the traditions that are perhaps less explicit than what you've been following. . . . I suppose the criticism that would be said, which isn't necessarily what I agree with, is that you only pick out what you want. You don't necessarily pick out the difficult bits and all the rest. You pick out the nice fluffy bits. I actually don't find that people who are creating their own spiritual path just pick out the nice fluffy bits. I think they're actually a lot more confronting of themselves than people who are sometimes in a very mainstream religion. . . . [It's about] finding clarity through different paths. But clarity is not something that is fluffy. Clarity is something that confronts you all the time with yourself, and with what's out there, with what you do, with what other people are as well. I mean one of the clichés about religion in general is that it's used as a crutch. It's like a nice thing to prop you up. And again that's not how I experience clarity at all. I experience it as something that constantly challenges me to look at myself with what I'm doing, with how I'm thinking especially. Yes, if it was just something soft and fluffy and making you feel nice, it might be nice to have now, but it's not actually really getting you anywhere.

Cathy's defence of her own 'pick-and-mix' religion rests on her view that it comes from a motivation to change herself, her practice and her ideas for the better, and her conviction that the variety of challenge she can access through the diversity of her practice and influences serves this aim better than the challenge she would receive in a mainstream religious environment. She suggests that, in her experience, people who construct their religious lives for themselves in this way often do so not as a way of avoiding uncomfortable challenge but as a way of seeking it out. As will be seen later, this view reflects well the self-reported attitudes of many individualized practitioners who have previously removed themselves from more formally institutional and/or hierarchical traditions. A less than charitable response might be to suggest that this reflects a self-justification of someone who does not want to admit that they found the structures and demands of institutional religion unacceptable. However, as will be seen in some of the accounts in this chapter, the main reason for leaving former affiliations is often not the demands made by religious institutions, but their perceived lack of ability to address the realities of participants' lives and/or their spiritual needs.

Groups, networks and centres of gravity

As I have already suggested, the majority of participants in this research have some kind of private religious practice conducted on their own, on a frequent and/or regular basis (Figure 9). However, their overall religious lives tend to be

Figure 9 Personal offering left in a nook in the wall of a derelict church in Heptonstall.

far from isolated. In and around the valley there are many religious, spiritual and creative groupings and shared activities available, and almost all of my participants are members or attenders of one or more of these. These spaces of engagement are independent of one another, and they vary widely in the forms that they take and the practices and ideas that they use. However, they are not completely self-contained, in that they do not require any kind of exclusivity of affiliation or commitment. While the specific affiliations, histories and practices on which they are predicated vary widely, they tend to have in common an assumption of a stance of openness, a lack of exclusivity and a low level of explicit requirements on practitioners in terms of beliefs or commitments. This means that individuals feel free to define their level and duration of involvement in any group or activity, and the place these associations have in their wider personal profiles of affiliations and practices. Arguably it is in part this sense of openness that makes these kinds of associations attractive to this population. It also means that there is significant crossover between those involved in the various activities.

These groups and activities themselves exist within the context of a wider set of overlapping networks that are best understood as constituting a spectrum of 'centres of religious gravity'. A centre of religious gravity is a cluster of groups, ideas and practices that feed off one another and have interrelated aims and ideas. Each centre of gravity provides a set of common ideas and structures, and a kind of internally recognized lingua franca that facilitates engagement between practitioners who involve themselves with it. These are very loose networks that tend to attract people with common experiences or ideas, and that revolve around generally accepted understandings and practices. There is no sense of firm membership, and often no hierarchical or institutional control of their activities. Levels and patterns of involvement of individuals in these centres of gravity vary widely, and it is very common for individuals to drift in and out of involvement with centres of gravity or to straddle multiple centres.

In later chapters I will explore in more detail the complexity of the relationships between individuals, groups, networks and centres of gravity. The rest of this chapter focuses on a more descriptive account of these relationships in the context of my participants, organized by the four centres of gravity that are most commonly relevant to the religious lives of my participants: Quakerism, non-aligned Buddhism, nature-based religion and women's spirituality. Clearly, there is insufficient space here to attempt a full account of each of these as religious contexts in their own right. These descriptions will therefore focus on the attitudes and motivations of participants towards the centres of gravity in which they involve themselves, and their relationships with their peers and with the groups and networks in which they participate.

Hebden Bridge Quaker Meeting

Five participants in this project are full members of the Hebden Bridge Quaker Meeting (HBQM), and another two either are or recently have been regular attenders. Of the seven, one was brought up within a Quaker family, and five either grew up in or had had significant involvement with various forms of Christianity before gravitating towards Quakerism as adults. For most, leaving Christianity was one decision, and becoming involved with Quakers was a separate, later decision, suggesting that there were both push and pull factors at play. Broadly, the reasons given by interviewees suggest first a feeling of being constricted by the way their former Christian denominations had understood, practised and organized religion, and then a consequent feeling that Quakerism allowed them more space to construct their own personal understanding of religion that they felt was right for themselves. For example, Naomi, a former Evangelical Christian, gives contrasting accounts of the two denominations she has been involved with:

> I formally finished it after working with missionaries in Peru. . . . I came back saying I can't do this anymore. Their God is definitely too small, and I can't do it. And whatever spirituality I have is larger than that. Or my idea of God is larger than that. So I decided I'd better not believe in God, if I couldn't just make up God to fit. So I'd better stop believing in God. So that was a big break for me because it had been a centre of my life for a long time. . . . I went off to the [Quaker Meeting] to see if there was a spiritual home I could go to. . . . It was wonderful. It was open. It was thoughtful. There were some people with quite a psychoanalytical approach, which I found useful. There were a lot of people there who had thought more deeply about things than me.

Naomi tells of a spiritual crisis moment, in which she perceived a mismatch between what she understood her spirituality as needing and the idea of spirituality being promulgated by the Christianity that had hitherto been very important in her life. She encompasses this feeling with the phrase 'My idea of God is larger than that', which suggests there is something that she needed more of. Like a number of other participants who have left traditional religious institutions, she was not unhappy with the idea of religion, but with the form of religion that was being offered. What she wanted more of is perhaps suggested by what she gives as her reasons for preferring Quakerism – more openness and more thoughtfulness.

Hugo's account of leaving Lutheranism and his later introduction to Quakerism strikes similar notes:

> I was brought up in the Lutheran Church. And then I read a book by Osho Bhagwan Rajneesh. . . . He talked about the Bible and he explained to me how Jesus can take our sins even though he died before us. And in the church they repeated it like a prayer, but nobody actually explained it to me. . . . I can't be complicit. That's against my convictions. So I had to leave. . . . I felt this was right. Not because I don't believe in God, but that's what Jesus would do. . . . [When I went to the Quaker Meeting] it was silence, which was nice. And then I just chatted with them about all sorts of things. And I mentioned extra-terrestrials and UFOs, and they actually listened. And you go to any other church, and you do this and people immediately move about one metre away from you, and internally make a cross, and say 'God save us from these weird things!' And I mean, these Quakers, they were happy as anything. They were open-minded. They listened to me. Absolutely tolerant. 'Oh, one of us is Buddhist, and another one is Pagan, and another one doesn't believe in Jesus but does his own things.' Perfect.

Megan further highlights the Quakers as a space in which she could acknowledge her sexuality openly:

> One of the things that impressed me was that they were talking about sexuality. And I'd had terrible trouble with mine. I wasn't out. . . . I thought that you know I would be cast out if I admitted anything. I was very confused about it all for a long, long time. . . . The Quakers did a book called *Towards a Quaker View of Sex*.[1] And it ran the gamut of 'actually all homosexual congress is wrong' to 'actually it's the quality of the relationship that's important and it doesn't matter what the genders of the people are'. And I thought 'I like that. That sounds my kind of thing.'

All three of these seem to have been attracted by their experience of Quakers as tolerant and inclusive of diversity. But in addition they were attracted by a sense that they would be encouraged and empowered to think for themselves, construct their own beliefs and practices for themselves, and so engage with a

---

[1] *Towards a Quaker View of Sex* was actually an essay written by a group of Quakers from London in 1963. It is available to download here: https://worldpolicy.org/wp-content/uploads/2010/04/Quak ers-1964-Towards-a-Quaker-View-of-Sex.pdf

wide range of potentially stimulating points of view. Indeed five of these seven interviewees are explicitly involved in one or more unrelated spiritual or religious activities in addition to their involvement with the Quakers, including Buddhism and Paganism and even Roman Catholicism in one case. The remaining two talk about their involvement in Quakerism as being about creating a diverse community with shared processes, rather than about commonality of belief. Una, a lifelong Quaker, puts it like this:

> My approach through the Meeting right from the early days, through my early experience with the young Quakers, has always been that we're all on a spiritual journey. I don't mind where your spiritual journey is coming from, is going to. But if you want to share the experience, let's do it together, and share it. And it doesn't matter if you go on somewhere else, or if you stay with us. So I've never been particularly concerned to badge it Quaker. I've more been interested in the way we do things as a way of enabling people to grow spiritually.

Una's comment suggests an investment in the idea that the religious lives and spiritual needs of others may be radically different to her own but also be equally valid and no less acceptable. Implicit in this relativistic approach, however, is also a sense that if others' concepts of religion are different then it would not be for them to impose those ideas on her. Underpinning it all is a desire for shared religious activity predicated on mutual stimulus and support.

Despite the openness to diversity of belief that appears common among Quaker participants, they nevertheless place value in what they see as a growing resource of tools, processes and wisdom dating back to early Quakerism and to George Fox. This is seen as a powerful legacy of the movement. Una's comment below illustrates how she values this legacy but without feeling confined by it:

> I'm quite keen that we don't want to lose the wisdom of the Quaker movement. However, I'm also completely happy to be outside the Quaker set up – in which case it's completely different mentally – do you know what I mean? So I do have – it's like two, two angles for me. The meeting is about two things. One is allowing people wherever they are, but creating structures that enable things to happen. You might need to pass on knowledge about – well, it's not just passing on knowledge, because somebody might have a better idea, but how we get to a way of sharing that enables you know, a good vessel. A good way of doing things. So sometimes that's made explicit, and we use Quaker tradition. But hey, if somebody's got a better idea for that moment, I'm completely open to that. . . . They're a set of resources that are growing all the time. Because that's one thing about Quakerism – it's moved a lot in its 350-odd years. It doesn't stay static. So it's open to fresh ideas coming through, or fresh light being shone or whatever.

Unlike Quaker groups in other nearby towns, HBQM chooses not to own its own building. Instead it holds what is termed 'Meeting for Worship' every Sunday morning in a hired room in a day care centre in the middle of Hebden Bridge. As Una suggests, the word worship is perhaps something of a misnomer for what is really the creation of a shared contemplative space:

> [The name Meeting for Worship] is a bit loaded. It's ancient I think. I think we need to move on. Meeting for Worship is a way of reaching. I think other people being in it help you reach a deeper place in yourself if it's working well. And the deeper I go, the more I trust what comes up.

The room in which Meeting for Worship is held is large, open and light. Chairs are arranged in a large circle, one to three rows deep. Meetings are attended by thirty to forty people, and follow a standard Quaker format of one hour's sitting in (mostly) silence during which testimony is given by members when they are moved to do so. This is followed by a brief period during which notices are read and reflections on the testimony are aired. Afterwards, there is tea and social mingling, and sometimes a talk or other activity for those who wish to stay on (Figure 10).

In addition to the Meeting for Worship, there are a number of other regular and group activities available for members to partake in, including

Figure 10 A post-meeting social event. Members of Hebden Bridge Quaker Meeting on a tour round Todmorden's Incredible Edible project.

guided meditation sessions using the Quaker 'Experiment With Light' shared meditation technique, and an annual residential weekend. There are also links to activities organized by and shared with Quakers from other meetings and other regions. HBQM has its own email newsletter, which is run by one of the members.

Members tend to see HBQM as 'lively' and 'somewhat alternative' compared with other Quaker groups in the region. This observation is generally viewed positively, although a couple of people who have experienced other meetings remarked that the amount of testimony and activity (people 'coming and going', etc.) during meetings can be off-putting. As one person put it to me,

> It can be that people speak because they want to speak rather than because they kind of divine the move to speak, if you like. And it sometimes feels like it's just a platform for people's personal views and personal experience.

This kind of attitude seems more common among those who grew up as Quakers or who have previously been longstanding members of other Quaker groups. It suggests a potential difference in experience between those who are more longstanding members and attenders and those who are relatively new to Quakerism.

Although five of those involved with HBQM are members, most don't see their identity as exclusively or even predominantly Quaker. As Naomi puts it,

> I would say that the Quaker Meeting grounds me, but I don't think of myself as primarily a Quaker. I think of myself as a person who attends and belongs to a Quaker Meeting. I think I'm bigger than that. . . . I would say I watch out for my spiritual life now, because for a time I didn't and it didn't go as well. And at the moment I'm very much part of the meeting. . . . But I don't consider that a big part of my identity I suppose. I don't know what I consider part of my identity, so that would be complicated anyway.

It is perhaps best to think of HBQM as a non-exclusive, affiliational and collaborative community with diffuse borders that is open to new members and casual visitors. The community is based around an offering of shared activities and opportunities for social and spiritual engagement. There are structures of organization based on rotating temporary leadership roles, which are intended to enable facilitation while minimizing top-down exercise of power. The Quaker Meeting has its own resource of formal and informal knowledge, which is intended to aid spiritual development, but the general attitude of members seems to be to avoid any sense of prescriptive doctrine or dogma.

Non-aligned Buddhists

In the recent past there have been a number of Buddhist groups and centres in and around the Upper Calder Valley, including branches of high profile traditions. Most significant among these was a local stately home called Dobroyd Castle,[2] which was bought by the New Kadampa Tradition (NKT) in 1995 and renamed as the Losang Dragpa Centre. This then served as a residential centre within the NKT for around twenty monks and nuns until it closed in 2007 amid allegations of unspecified impropriety.[3] Today, among others, there is a Dechen Kagyu Centre in Macphela Mill on the Burnley Road[4] and a Soto Zen group that meets on a weekly basis at the Calderdale and Blessingway Yoga Centres (see Figure 11).[5] There are also numerous groups and activities that are not specifically Buddhist but make use of Buddhist ideas and meditation techniques.

Five of my research participants characterize their religious lives as either significantly or primarily Buddhist in nature. Although all five of these have in the past had direct instruction from (and in two cases ordination within) specific Buddhist and Buddhist-derived traditions, including NKT, Triratna,[6] Soto Zen, The Thai Forest Tradition and others, none of them admits of any current or ongoing affiliation. Rather, all see themselves as working independently outside of any traditions. This self-identity as a non-aligned Buddhist seems then to be a not uncommon stance in the area. While the role of Buddhism in the personal religions of these five varies, there are some common elements, four of which are highlighted later.

First, each of the five describes themselves as having undergone a process of moving away from Christianity and towards Buddhism. Three were raised as Roman Catholics. The other two were raised as atheists and then became for a time actively involved in (respectively) Evangelical and Orthodox Christian traditions, before then moving on to Buddhism. One of these, Zena, describes her decision to follow Buddhism over Christianity:

> I just felt this need, for some reason, to follow a spiritual path. It was just a real drive. And so at the point where I was weighing and choosing which way, and the traditional conventional religion of my country is Christian Orthodoxy and Buddhism. And basically, it became Buddhism, after much consideration.

---

2   A stately home situated in the hills above Todmorden.
3   See: https://www.todmordennews.co.uk/news/castle-mystery-as-monks-quit-1-1841581
4   See: http://www.dechen.org/buddhist-centres/hebdenbridge/
5   See: http://hebdenbridgezen.org.uk
6   Formerly known as FWBO or Friends of the Western Buddhist Order.

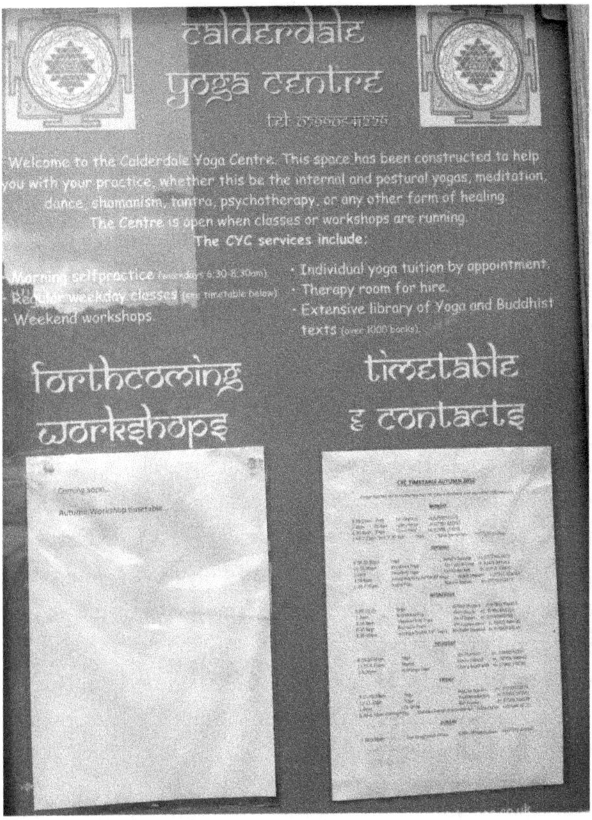

Figure 11 Calderdale Yoga Centre is one of numerous spaces bookable for yoga, meditation and other groups. The centre runs sessions for 'self practice', and has a library of yoga and Buddhist texts available for use.

It is interesting that Zena frames her decision to embrace Buddhism in two ways. On the one hand she talks of having felt a 'real drive', which speaks of a force outside of her control leading her towards a 'spiritual path', perhaps resulting from some aspect of herself or from some kind of irresistible attractor. On the other hand, she presents her move as a completely rational process of selection. She seems to be suggesting that she felt a need and then rationally thought through what would fill this need. The reasons given by the other four participants for rejecting Christianity all revolve around two strands. One, exemplified by three statements made by Ros, is a dislike of their particular Christian institution, and consequently of institutionalization more generally:

> Dislike for religious institutions really, and I think that's a bit of damage that the Catholic Church did to me. I don't like institutionalized religion. I'm more

friends with it than I was, but there's an awful lot about it that I don't like. . . .
I'm not very comfortable with the way in which religions get involved in the
machinations and apparatus of the state. And I think the Catholic Church
opened my eyes to that, because it is fairly stark. . . . I don't want to have any kind
of religion that says that men are better than women. And even some Buddhists
say that men are better than women. Well they can stuff it up their arse, really.
That was one of the things that made me get pissed off with the Catholic Church.
I just thought it was ridiculous, really, that attitude towards women.

The other strand, as exemplified by Victor, constitutes a claim of having reached
a point of feeling that Christianity as practiced and understood in their religious
situation was not adequate to meet their personal spiritual needs:

> The change away from Catholicism came when I was about 20. I needed to talk
> to somebody about [my spiritual experiences], and I went to talk to the local
> priest. And the priest just told me I was the devil. Like, you know, I could see
> the oneness of things, and that life was all the one life, as I would call it now. . . .
> [But] I was the devil, basically. And that was it. That was me and Christianity
> finished. . . . And of course, you know, he didn't point me towards *The Cloud
> of Unknowing*, or Padre Pio, or any of the Christian mystics. Not at all. It was
> just his limited small-minded Catholicism. There's plenty of scope within
> Christianity for true experience.

In different ways and to varying extents, all five exhibit both these strands, which
also seem similar to the reasons given by members of the Quaker Meeting for
rejecting their previous institutional Christian affiliations. While the sequence
of transformation may have varied, there appears a general pattern of both a
push and a pull – a wish to move away from institutionalization, together with a
wish to move towards practices, ideas or experiences that subjectively feel more
expansive and/or spiritually rewarding.

The second common element is that while these participants tend to talk
about Buddhism as something like a philosophical foundation, they give a sense
of building their individualized personal religion on top of that, and of being
open to a wide range of sources and influences in doing so. As Cathy puts it,

> When you're in the NKT, you're only really supposed to read books within that
> tradition. It's very defined in that way. And all other Buddhism is evil and will
> only lead you astray. It's the only pure tradition. So when I came out of that, I
> started off by reading more about other Buddhist traditions, in particular Zen. . . .
> And then starting studying with the Open University and getting references
> to different books that I could pick up on and follow, and then to Amazon

and looking at what recommendations came up from them. And lots and lots of reading. Eckhart Tolle was a big influence for a while, and then getting, I suppose, a lot of other post New Age, and recognising a lot there on non-duality. I also watched a lot of the Big Mind Zen videos that were online.[7] . . . it's just deliberately following things up. Like I read about Gnosticism for quite a while, and early Christianity. . . . The influences of Buddhism and Christianity are very important. . . . I've integrated some definite Christian elements in. I wouldn't call myself a Christian, but that's because I don't agree with the Church and what the Church does. But I'm quite happy to use the Christian things, the Christian imagery. And I'm also at the point where it doesn't matter to me how much is true about the Christian story or not. It's a useful way of looking at things. . . . Christianity has been an interest. But Buddhism is a very important foundation as well. It's a good foundation for anything in terms of spirituality.

The third common element is that while these participants generally express positivity about the idea of religious teachers, they specifically describe relationships with teachers in which they themselves maintain ongoing conscious control over whom they accept as teacher, the extent of contact and the extent to which they accept teachings. Paavo, for example, talks about what makes a good teacher:

They usually call themselves a teacher or a guru. Could be anyone. He just sits in front. You give him your seven pounds. And we call him a spiritual teacher. You almost allow him to be the spiritual teacher. But what makes a spiritual teacher [is] if they seem to know something about themselves. Not knowing anything about me. It's about knowing about them. If I get a sense that they know about themselves and they're not trying to find out about me. Then if they know themselves, they've much more of a chance of me finding out who I am. But if the spiritual teacher's trying to tell me who I am, then I run a mile. . . . Anybody is capable of being a teacher. Everyone's got that quality about them. We all learn from each other, if you're open to learning. Not learning from everything that people say to you, but you take the best from somebody. You know, you're in the taxi one day and the taxi driver is talking lovingly about his wife, and you think 'Ah, sweet'. You know, that's a lesson that we can all learn. It's just something you take on. You know you take on something positive. For him, he doesn't know that he's being a teacher. But for me in that moment he is a teacher.

In this quote Paavo veers between two senses of what a teacher is. In the first sense, a teacher is somebody who claims to be a teacher, and often might require something in return from those whom they teach – whether it be attention,

---

[7] Videos produced by an American Zen teacher, Dennis Paul Merzel (also known as Genpo Roshi), which are available online via: http://bigmind.org/video.

payment or whatever. Judging from the language he uses, perhaps in his experience this kind of teacher has often tended to be male. In the second sense, everybody that he meets is a potential teacher, whose potential is realized if and to the extent that he learns something valuable from his encounter with them. There is in this sense of teaching no transaction, and no requirements made on the learner. His juxtaposition of these two senses of what it is to be a teacher suggests that teachers who claim objective knowledge (that are 'trying to tell me who I am') are the kind of teacher that is to be avoided. He is prepared (he suggests) to give the attention or the payment and accept somebody as a teacher (on a contingent basis) if he perceives them to be a good teacher. His criteria for this is simple and based around subjectivity. If they have good subjective awareness of themselves and their own religious perspective, then like the accidental teachers of the second sense they may be a good teacher and worth the interaction and the payment.

While some non-aligned Buddhists in the sample do have face-to-face relationships with teachers, others learn about Buddhism and Buddhist practice through books, online videos or other indirect sources. Arguably one of the attractions of this mode of learning is that it gives themselves an even greater level of personal control over what instruction to receive and what to accept.

Fourth and finally, while all five of these participants do engage in various meditative, reflective or devotional practices that appear to be derived from and/ or reference Buddhism, their practice tends to favour subjective perceptions of utility over purity of adherence to any traditional orthopraxy. Two of the five indicate that they regard the spending of time alone walking in the woods as an active meditative activity, and a third is a self-taught Buddhist artist who regards her art as her primary Buddhist practice. Another describes her religious practice as including both Buddhist meditation and Shamanic drumming, while the other regularly attends the Quaker Meeting.

While these people are not current insiders within Buddhist traditions, and are comfortable working outside traditions' norms and rules, they are also neither casual nor uneducated in their utilization of Buddhist ideas and practices. All have gone through similar routes comprising rejection of institutionalization alongside an embracing of Buddhist philosophies, often alongside other forms of spirituality.

Nature-based and animistic religion

Around half of my participants describe their religion in terms that might be understood as Pagan and/or animist. Of these, about a third practise as Shamans, and one identified herself specifically as a witch. Together they are a significant but diverse subculture around nature-based religion, with multiple centres of gravity.

Many of the participants who describe their religion in Pagan or animist terms are also longstanding residents of the valley, some of whom have lived in or near Hebden Bridge since the 1970s. Some brought their interest in Paganism with them to the area (having previously lived in Glastonbury or other centres of alternative spirituality), and there is an apparent shared history of Paganism among these and others in the valley that goes back to the original hippy influx. This is a history of development of ideas among the participants, and also of the formation of groups and networks that have followed their own life cycles as their members' lives developed, before disbanding or dissolving and so giving way to successor initiatives. A remark of Diane's about a group that had existed for over fifteen years invokes a flower analogy to suggest a group whose function grew over time, but with a natural lifespan that meant moving on once this function started to be fulfilled: 'So it sort of dynamically grew, and then wilted if you like (laughs).'

Especially in the 1980s and 1990s but also up to the present day, groups and networks have brought people together to collaborate over and share ritualistic and non-ritualistic Pagan practice in the countryside around Hebden Bridge. These groups as recounted by participants have varied in their size, their make-up (e.g. one was a women's only group, while others were mixed), and in their particular emphases (e.g. one participant describing how one group in the 1980s changed from being purely ritual to being more psychotherapeutic in focus).

One such group was comprised of friends who originally got together to investigate ley lines. Steve describes the range of activities of this group:

> We used to go all over, because in a four-wheel drive you can go anywhere. We used to go all over the North of England. And we used to make regular trips to Glastonbury at the Spring equinox, particularly. We used to mark the Celtic year. But ley hunting was a way of getting out and about, because we were finding things. We were a very interesting bunch of people, all doing different things, really. But this is how we spent some of our leisure time – poring over maps, thinking 'I can see a straight line between that church and that tor, and that whatever.' And we'd just go out and investigate things.

In common with other accounts, this quote suggests a group that was very open, informal and non-exclusive, and whose function for its members was a mix of the religious, the social, the recreational and the exploratory. One could quite easily imagine that different members of this group found value in its activities in very different ways. Reports suggest that it never really ended, but became progressively looser and less active as its members got older. Today, many seem to be still local, still in contact and still friends. Some of them are now variously involved with a group based around a locally produced earth mysteries magazine called Northern Earth, and still travel out together on trips to stone circles and natural features.[8]

In addition to these more peer-led groups, there is also a wide variety of facilitated groups and activities available around nature-based spiritualities. These include activities such as sweat lodges, fire walking and so on. Again, the motivation for these seems to be a mix of the social and the spiritual, and there appears to be at least one social subculture revolving around such activities. While they are often advertised on Facebook, websites and through leaflets and notices in local shops, they are also quite often set up and communicated through discussion and word of mouth at other social or spiritual events. Different events are led by different people, and there are a number of individuals that have what might be called a high spiritual reputation, such that their events will tend to be well attended. Here, Owen talks about the general scene and about how one particular sweat lodge was organized:

> There are still spiritual things going on in the area. And there are people who I know from way back who are doing these things. And I link into those. I'm going to a sweat lodge on Sunday. A Beltane sweat lodge run by an old friend. One of the originals. And I'm looking forward to it. A mixed sweat lodge as well. So that'll be good. Because I knew she was doing women's sweat lodges, so I badgered her a bit, and said 'when are you doing a mixed one?' And that's about purification. Renewal and reflection.

By 'One of the originals', what Owen means is somebody who (like himself) came to the valley as part of the hippy influx of the 1970s. This is somebody whom he has therefore known for over forty years. On his account this particular sweat lodge was instituted due to a discussion between himself and his friend, and he suggests that what he will get out of the event will be a mixture of social and spiritual benefits.

It is important to note, however, that while participants often do partake in groups such as these, much of the Pagan and nature-based activity that they

---

[8]   See http://www.northernearth.co.uk

describe has been and is undertaken on an individual and personal basis. For example, Andy describes how his practice to mark the rituals of the Pagan wheel of the year, and consequently also his religious identity, have changed over time:

> It used to be primarily the eight times a year. Well I still acknowledge those festivals, but the big difference is that it is kind of 'What are you on about, eight times a year? It's every day!' [laughs]. It's every day you've got to have this consciousness – which is when I stopped calling myself a Pagan as such, because that seems to be based around certain ritual times. I realized it's a lifestyle. It's a way of thinking.

Implicit in Andy's account is a sense that what for him were once more formally scheduled rituals conducted on traditional Pagan festivals and perhaps with others, have gradually transformed into a more personal and private kind of practice. While once doing something on the right day with the right people might have mattered more, he is suggesting that what has become more important for him now is to maintain a feeling of connection with the seasons on an ongoing basis. This seems to be symbolized for him by the dropping of the 'Pagan' label.

Animism, understood as reference to the world as containing not just human but also non-human persons that can be experienced and related to (Harvey, 2005, xi), is common among this group of participants. Entities to which people admitted relating as to non-human persons ranged from the valley as an entity in its own right to spirits of particular areas or aspects of the landscape, to spirit guides in animal form. For some animism is perhaps a fairly casual way of expressing a feeling of being subject to outside agency, as exemplified by Hugo:

> I call it maybe the spirit of Hebden Bridge. And I feel like there's something. You know, this, the spirit is very strong. And, if you take the risk, the universe supports you.

A number of people who talked about animistic experiences or stances sought to qualify their claims by making any link between their experiences and external metaphysical realities contingent. This also perhaps illustrates a tendency for individuals in this kind of subculture to claim as ordinary an innate ability to sense and relate to such entities.

A significant number of participants have spent much time studying in pursuit of their religion. Some, like Kate, have spent years following training paths offered by teachers and groups in Shamanic practice, or in specific mystery traditions:

> I'm going back to being a teenager now. I sort of became more animist, I suppose, in my outlook. Then I explored yoga, Tai Chi, and they in a way helped me on

my path. Meditation. I then started looking into what you can find out about the old ways. Roughly Pagan you could call it. Trying to look at what was left (which wasn't much) of Celtic Spirituality or Wicca. . . . The strongest thing for me was my introduction to the Medicine Wheel teachings,[9] which began with a sweat lodge. That was back in the eighties. . . . It just felt to me a very at home place. It resonated with me on a deep level, the sweat lodge ceremony. So I started to explore that. And I met some teachers in the Medicine Wheel tradition at that time. I didn't really follow it much in the eighties because I was already studying to be [and] practicing as a herbalist. . . . So that kind of got shelved but it was always there. And then later I came back to the Medicine Wheel tradition in about 2000. I came back to it again and studied more. And I've studied it very intensively since about 2009. A different tradition. . . . And the same with my work as well. I trained in plant spirit medicine. That was very influential as well. So that's working in a Shamanic way with the spirits of the plants.

Kate seems to be describing a sense of having charted her own journey of spiritual exploration through contact with and involvement in various streams. Some of these – notably the Medicine Wheel teachings and herbalism – constitute curricula that she felt herself at the time (and still does in retrospect) to have been beneficial in giving her the stimulus, support and learning that she needed at that time. Others (notably her early meditation and her ongoing involvement in sweat lodge ceremonies) seem to be presented as stopping off points, or temporary homes, that have enabled her to progress through practice. Overall, she frames this journey as something that she has been in control of, even when under the tuition of others, but in which the stimuli and ideas she has come across have been of sometimes great and lasting influence.

As a strand of activity in the valley, nature-based and animist religious sentiment and practice seem widespread and diverse. It plays a very different role in different people's lives, but tends to have strongly social as well as spiritual overtones. For some there are also strong political overtones, which support various forms of activism (see Figure 12). This is exemplified by this quote from Liam:

There are very many people here who are very committed to and sophisticated in their spiritual practice. And many of them are involved in environmental and social change work in some way. . . . And there's very powerful and compelling evidence that traditional spiritual customs, norms and beliefs. . . . play vital structural roles in terms of human relationship with the environment and the practical and material outcomes of that.

[9] A group of lineage traditions, including that promulgate teachings modelled on Native American spirituality.

Figure 12 Anti-fracking benefit gig in the Trades Club, Hebden Bridge.

Liam talks about the beliefs, customs and norms of traditional land-based spirituality as being in part a repository of knowledge and wisdom about land management. He frames the valley as a kind of living laboratory, where this wisdom can be uncovered and put to use. Elsewhere he suggests that this occurs not just through the activities of Neopagans, but through a wider set of informal networks that facilitate information exchange and productive contact between Neopagans, earth scientists and environmental activists who are concerned with issues such as climate change and the fight against fracking.

Goddess and women's spirituality

Around half of the women participants in this research brought up 'Goddess spirituality' or 'women's spirituality' as being a significant (to varying degrees) part of their personal religious story. This includes women of various religious identities, including for example both Quakers and Pagans. A number linked their interest back to their participation in the Women's Movement of the 1970s and 1980s, or to consciousness raising and other women's groups formed and active during that time. Some specifically mentioned a Women's Spirituality

Group that existed for about 15 years in the 1980s and 1990s in Hebden Bridge. Kate is a typical example:

> I was in the Women's Spirituality Group and we were a matriarchy study group back in the '80s, so we were exploring the Goddess from all different cultures. So that was quite an exploration of the feminine.

One of the common themes underpinning interest in the idea of women's spirituality is a notion that women tend to have a particular capacity for spirituality (or perhaps for particular kinds of spirituality), and for making a positive difference to the world through spiritual practice. Emma puts it like this:

> I've never stopped teaching, learning, sharing, caring. It's, you know, the archetypically female traits, but also the ones that are making change. And I do believe it is women that have got far greater capacity to make these connections.

Becks goes further, relating this to a particular capacity among women for relating in a mutually supportive way:

> It's really important for women to come into space. And I think women are naturally able to do this better, to share the space, and to get into this kind of deep bonding with each other. And this starts to generate ideas, and ideas that can change society as well.

Both of these quotes set up a certain kind of spirituality as being around creating connections of empathy, and of creating power (specifically the power to change society for the better) through these connections (see also Figure 13). They both assign the ability to create these connections as a specifically female ability, relating it to activities of sharing, bonding and nurturing. They both implicitly suggest a responsibility (not necessarily a responsibility that falls on women but perhaps one that women are seen as well suited to meet) to engage in this kind of activity as a service to one another and to the world. However in both quotes, this wider responsibility is seen perhaps as a corollary of rather than a direct driver towards the creation of networks of bonding and nurturing as a good in their own right.

Another common theme is the idea that women have become alienated from their spirituality by patriarchy, and consequently therefore have a need to reclaim it. In this quote, for example, Becks suggests a long history of societal, structural and institutional restrictions on women's ability to pursue their spirituality:

> A lot of the work I do is just with women, because women need to reclaim their spirituality really. Well, since 500 AD, when the Roman Emperor decided women could no longer be priestesses, and were impure and all of that.

Figure 13 An angel mosaic, screwed onto a wall in Todmorden town centre. The image depicts a female angel figure with a prominent heart.

Elsewhere, she suggests that women can find themselves restricted through the mechanics of gendered personal interaction:

> I am actually now opening up to working with men, but I've had to go through a long process of strengthening myself so I don't respond to men in the way you've been programmed to respond, and to be able to stand in my own power and not kind of give that away. We're just so prone to looking for someone outside ourselves to take the lead or to tell us what to do or to be the authority.

Women's spirituality, then, is often seen by participants as an act of exploration of female experience and identity, a pioneering of different ways of relating and being, and as a reclamation of power both for personal benefit and for the wider good. Some, like Una, linked their interest in women's spirituality with their own past involvement in the wider Women's Movement in the 1970s and 1980s:

> I got very involved with the Women's Movement and exploring that area, and spiritual stuff as well. . . . There was a women's non-violent direct action group.

You know, that wasn't a religious thing at all, but I'm still in touch with a couple of people from that, from thirty-five years ago. And setting up the Well Women Centre. I'm still in touch with women I worked with in that phase, where we shared a line of travel. Even though they're not religious as such.

This suggests the existence of a much wider set of networks rooted in these past activities. It also hints at a political connection, further evidenced in the way some such as Emma talk about their past involvement in peace camps and direct action:

The highlights of my life have been the things I'm talking about. The Women's Spirituality Group. Greenham. All the peace actions have been with women, mainly, and often lesbians, who have had to really look at what the world does to people and look for alternative ways.

Two particular sources of inspiration are evident. The first is the concept of Goddess (described here by Diane):

A sort of Celtic or native British spirituality may reflect upon a goddess like Bridget or Bridie. But it's because you may be seeking to find a connection within yourself with those attributes. So I might put a picture of Bridget up or get a sprig of a Rowan tree to represent Bridget. But actually what I'm doing is having a visual conception of what I'm seeking to find from within. I don't actually think there's ever been an actual goddess called Bridget roaming around. I think it's been a concept.

A second source of inspiration is the social history of women in the local area (again here discussed by Diane):

When this was shaped into a mill town there was a disproportionate amount of women working, being quite dynamic. . . . The first women's guild was set up here, to do with the unions and fighting for your rights. Similarly, the suffragette movement. . . . Women had to work to help each other. . . . Although that industrialization has gone, we have a new wave of networking and women standing up for themselves. . . . So as I've learnt more about the history of the place, and the strong women who I've identified, it makes me very proud to remain part of this place. And to carry on the tradition in a different way.

Participants interpret their interest in and activity relating to women's spirituality in various ways, but often it involves the creation of small women-only groups of various kinds, with an intention of nurturing close relationships. Becks, who is also involved in various other women's spirituality initiatives, describes one such group of which she is a member, and which is Shamanic in focus:

It's all very non-hierarchical. We're a group of four women. We all bring our gifts and talents to that group. . . . And this is the thing I love about where I'm at now. It's about your experience as an individual. But then you see your experience mirrored in the other people around you, which creates very strong bonds of community because it's based on empathy, and understanding each other at a deep level.

Regular practice and ritual groups

Many participants are active members of groups that meet on a regular basis with specific practice aims. Very often this aim is a shared practice that, for each of the group's members, is just one element of their religious activity. There are numerous such groups active in the area and they tend to be open, non-exclusive and fluid in their membership. They last for varying amounts of time. Below are brief accounts of two example groups.

A Taizé Harmony Singing Group[10] meets in a private house a few minutes walk from Hebden Bridge town centre every Tuesday morning. Each session lasts around one hour and would normally be attended by between six and fifteen people, there being a core of six to eight regular attenders, a larger pool of occasional attenders (many of whom live outside of Hebden Bridge and attend when visiting the area) and sometimes one or two first-timers. The sessions are informal, open and relaxed in tone. The general structure of the sessions is that participants sit in a circle on chairs in the living room, and sing a series of multi-part devotional songs in the Taizé style, alternated with short periods of silence in which a feeling of quiet reflection tends to prevail. Which tunes are sung is normally decided through requests from participants (many of whom know most of the songs and have their own favourites). Some of the participants are good singers with musical training, although there are also singers who are unconfident and/or relatively unmusical. There are no expectations apparent in terms of ability to sing, and the good singers often tend to take it upon themselves to encourage or even help those who are less confident. The chants are mostly Christian or influenced by Christianity, although none of the usual participants regard themselves as primarily Christian.

---

[10] Taizé singing is a style of multi-part devotional harmonic singing popularized by the Taizé Christian monastic community in France (https://www.taize.fr/en_rubrique2603.html). A short video of Hebden Bridge Taizé Harmony Singing Group is available to watch at https://www.youtube.com/watch?v=K76PM1OtMaU.

There is no significant sharing of doctrine or belief, and very little discussion of spirituality at or associated with the Taizé sessions. However, those who take part do talk about the sessions as a specifically spiritual activity, and as a shared spiritual activity, as exemplified by Cathy:

> The Taizé group doesn't tend to discuss spirituality. We do it rather than discuss it. So the fact that we do it is important. But there's no limitation. I mean you can come to a Taizé group just because you like singing if you want to, but I assume people generally don't, because the silence is there as well.

Often after sessions, participants typically stay on for coffee – creating a regular but also impromptu social event that often lasts an hour or more. Discussion during coffee often revolves around what other spiritual or related events are going on, the social news from the wider networks of members, and sometimes current affairs.

Events called Deep Sound Gong Baths are run on Wednesday lunchtimes and occasional Saturday evenings by a small collective that calls itself the Deepsong Gong Sacred Sound Collective.[11] The Wednesday sessions are held in Calderdale Yoga Studio in the centre of Hebden Bridge and are an hour long. They attract up to fifty or so participants, who typically lie on yoga mats with blankets and pillows in relative darkness, while the session leader creates a shifting soundscape intended to promote relaxation and meditation. The collective's website lists as instruments used to create this soundscape: 'gongs, crystal and Tibetan bowls,[12] wind-chimes, bells, shruti box,[13] chanting, toning, drumming, Solfeggio frequencies,[14] and loving silence.' Saturday sessions are run in the evening in a basement yoga studio half way up one of the hills on the outskirts of Hebden Bridge, and is run on similar lines but is smaller, and with perhaps a more intimate feel.

During the session the participants are passive recipients, who understand themselves as gaining benefit from being subjected to and experiencing the soundscape that is produced. As one participant put it:

> I feel as if they're almost like a substitute for going to church – the sort of inspirational aspect of just listening to the amazing sound that the gongs make, and putting you into a state of meditation. And then there are the readings or poetry, which are often on themes connected with peace.

---

[11] See http://www.deepsong.org/D_%20collective.html#Collective
[12] Tibetan singing bowl: a kind of upturned bell that can be played singly or continuously.
[13] Shruti box: an Indian instrument similar to a harmonium, used to provide a steady drone.
[14] Solfeggio frequencies: a set of specific notes defined by their frequency, said to have healing and other beneficial properties.

The gong baths, then, have some characteristics of a religious service. However, as with the Taizé singing sessions there is no doctrine or belief requirement, although there are doubtless beliefs that are generally shared, especially with respect to the claimed healing properties and other value of sacred sound. And as with the Taizé sessions there is leadership, but a kind of light touch leadership that sees itself as providing an open service for participants to make use of, rather than making requirements on them. As one of the members of the collective puts it,

> There are special people in Hebden Bridge, who have this special sensitivity. And that means that on the other side of the coin they're quite vulnerable. And they need these places, these oases that they can go to and recharge their batteries. I call it relax, renew and reach for your dreams. But even that sounds a bit pretentious to me, because I don't know what it's doing. You can look at the research on sound. To play the gongs for an hour. Sound moves matter. And I know but I've been doing this for years now. And I've had all sorts of different feedback from people about the benefits. So some people come out of there feeling very tranquil. Others have come out of there with relief from pain that they've had for a long, long time. And there's others that it contacts their fear and it's disturbing to them. Some want it louder. Others want it more quiet. So I tend to go from a kind of respect of all comers. Everybody is welcome and they get what they get from it. What I do is to try and make it coming from love.

After the Wednesday sessions, many of the participants go together to Marco's (the local café mentioned in Chapter 3), where they drink coffee and talk for much of the afternoon. This is a highly informal and relaxed but regular social event that is well attended by participants and by others who have not been present at the gong bath.

The Open Shamanic Journeying Circle takes place on Thursday evenings at the Energy Centre, a space set aside for spiritual activity in an office building in the middle of Hebden Bridge. Sessions are presented as for both beginners and more experienced practitioners, and typically have three to four participants plus the leader. They start with a ritual of 'aura-cleansing' conducted by the session leader using smoke from a burning bundle of sage called a 'smudge' stick (a practice borrowed from Native American tradition, Figure 14). Participants then declare personal intentions for the meeting. These are typically to answer a question or gain enlightenment on a particular issue. The session consists of two 'journeys', which vary in form but usually involve a period of Shamanic drumming in a darkened environment, during which participants claim to access trance states through which they can encounter and engage with spirit guides. After each journey, participants recount their experiences to the group. Some also record

Figure 14 A smudge stick. These bundles of dried sage are used in Shamanic Journeying sessions to create scented smoke for the ritual of aura-cleansing.

them in personal journey diaries. Unlike the other sessions mentioned earlier, there is little direct social activity around these sessions.

These kinds of groups clearly perform some of the functions that institutionalized religion performs, especially with respect to the social and therapeutic aspects of religious practice. However, they do seek to do this without making the same requirements in terms of affiliation, allegiance or doctrinal assent and by maintaining but drawing on non-hierarchical concepts of leadership and authority (as will be discussed in detail in Chapters 6 and 7). Virtually all of my research participants are or (in a couple of cases) have recently been members of such groups, and have different profiles of membership as they choose to suit their own personal practice. While these groups could be framed as a service that is being provided to members, it perhaps seems most appropriate to think of them primarily in terms of self-sustaining social circles.

Centres of gravity within the community

In discussing the religious frameworks in which my participants operate, I have focused on the notion of 'centres of gravity' and given a brief description of four of these centres of gravity that are important in the religious lives of these individuals.

A centre of gravity is best thought of as a linked set of shared ideas, cultural norms and commonly accepted spheres of engagement, which attracts individuals into its orbit, but at the same time is dynamically formed by their presence and actions. The term 'centres of gravity' is deliberately chosen, since it suggests a theoretical centre around which numerous entities revolve, which is itself created by their presence, their behaviour and their mutual sense of attraction. It is important to note that the interactions between those involved with a centre of gravity are likely to be very diverse, and need not conform to any set of rules, formal or informal. It is quite possible for specific individuals involved in the same centre of gravity to never encounter one another, but it is also possible within a centre of gravity for close relationships and groups to form and to disband. The complexity of relationships and how they evolve over time affect the relative importance of specific individuals and specific groups within the overall cultural landscape.

The four centres of gravity that I have described are markedly different from one another not only in their core ideas and practices but also in the extent to which those involved with them engage with one another and the ways in which they do so. However, at the same time they are affected by one another's parallel existence and by ongoing crossover between them over time. The only one that has a formal membership structure is the Quaker Meeting, but even in that case it is not uncommon for individuals to be heavily involved in the centre of gravity while remaining outside of the formal structure. The centre of gravity with the lowest level of engagement between its local members is the non-aligned Buddhists, but even in this case there is mutual engagement through structures ranging from links of friendship to membership of practice groups, and a shared understanding through engagement with a relatively stable set of core principles and ideas that transcends the local community. Each of the four centres of gravity is grounded in part in its own hinterland of shared experiences and activities over the years, which in each case has led to its own set of mutual understandings, commonly but loosely held among those within its orbit. All four of these centres of gravity have existed in the local area for decades, but without fixed membership or institutional hierarchical control. The practice and ritual groups in which practitioners involve themselves may be functionally close to one particular centre of gravity, or to more than one, or to none.

A multiplicity of routes

The earlier sections cover the most commonly held memberships, affiliations and practices among my participants. However, two general points must be made with respect to these. First, while it is common for participants in this project to engage with one or more of these four centres of gravity, the ways in which they choose to do so are extremely diverse. Second, and relatedly, in the town as a whole there is a much wider range of activities going on, which are reflected in the range of themes that came up in participant accounts. Some connected themselves in discussion with established churches or organizations with national or international scope, as either members or affiliates. One participant combines Quakerism with regular attendance at Roman Catholic Mass and is also involved in several Catholic-led ecumenical initiatives. Others are members of groups relating to Anthroposophy, Sufism, Subud, non-violent communication, 5Rhythms and so on.

Membership of groups tends to be finite, even sometimes quite ephemeral. A number of participants in this project have formerly been involved with various groups and activities and then made conscious decisions to discontinue their involvement. Sometimes this was because of a feeling that the group no longer worked for them personally, but the reason might equally have been simply a matter of convenience, as exemplified by Ros:

> I did make a brief foray into 5Rhythms. Which isn't really a religion. It's a method. I did that for about five years, quite seriously, and it was a big part of my life. But it is a method, and it does involve a lot of self-reflection, ultimately. And I reflected on the fact that I was doing too much, and thought 'What sort of things are there that I'm doing that I don't need to do, that could make my life more open?' And I thought 'Oh, 5Rhythms!' [laughs] So I stopped doing it! That's the silliness, but that's the truth. That is what happened. It was the one thing I absolutely didn't have to do. And so I stopped.

Examples such as this suggest that the way participants have organized their spiritual engagement is often as much as anything a case of fitting in with the demands of other aspects of their lives. But this example illustrates well how easily participants feel they can move in and out of groups and affiliations, how there is therefore a kind of drifting of individuals between groups, and how this often is related to a subjective sense of personal control. Arguably, in this case Ros moved on from 5Rhythms precisely because she felt her involvement in it had given her what she wanted from it.

It should be clear from this chapter so far that each participant in this study has a unique profile of religious views, ideas, sensibilities and practices, and that they perceive this as being under their own control. Each also has their own understanding of the way their religious activity fits into their wider lives, and the linkages and boundaries between their religion and their other activities. For example, Zena describes the connections between her personal religion and her musical practice:

> Frame drumming is a sacred practice. A frame drum is an instrument sacred to Goddess. So this is like the practical side of things. . . . Music is spiritual. . . . The time when we rehearse is one of the times when I feel most alive, creative, engaged, connected. Just alive, basically. . . . Music is this intense opportunity, that doorway into heightened consciousness and reality.

Ros describes how art contributes to her own Buddhist practice:

> Creating and producing Buddhist art is just another way of focusing on the principles of the religion. There's many different ways of personifying them and making them part of your life. And creating art is just one way of doing so. Because . . . when you're doing art you're contemplating it quite a lot. And there are many ways in which the aesthetics of Buddhist art contribute to one's understanding of the message of Buddhism and the core beliefs and so on.

Quinn tells how spiritual searching led her to see storytelling as her primary practice:

> In the seventies I went and got involved in every alternative thing going, and read the Bible cover to cover and went to India. That was my thing. I was driven to find out what more there was in life. And I felt wrong in myself. Wanted to feel right. And I searched all over the place. And coming to storytelling was part of that search. And has satisfied me more than any of those other things, strangely.

In Quinn's case, whether it makes sense to call her storytelling a religious, secular or spiritual practice is perhaps something of a moot point, dependent on one's precise definition of religion. However, in discussing a phenomenon as diverse as individualized religion, it would seem inappropriate to draw arbitrary definitional boundaries to exclude this kind of activity. This also applies to the two participants who defined themselves as Humanist. One, Grace, is a poet and writer who also acts as a Humanist funeral celebrant, and the other, Xia, described the 'Spirit of Hebden Bridge' as marking out her own community, culture and value set.

Conclusion

Religious culture among this population is rich, creative and diverse. Each participant maintains their own unique profile of engagement, allegiance, practice and belief, rooted in their own prior history and influences. Each feels free to define for themselves in what their spirituality or religion consists, and how it relates to and informs their overall lives. However, and despite this highly individualized stance, these people are by no means isolated from one another with respect to their religion. Most have multiple and often overlapping spheres of engagement and affiliation, which they actively use to enable an approach that is experimental and exploratory, but that also feeds the development and expression of values that are common in the valley but that they also perceive to be their own. Ideals of sharing and mutual support are held as important by this population, but at the same time, there is a widely felt aversion to any possibility of subjection to hierarchical or institutional control. This is, then, a culture that prioritizes both the individual and community at the same time. The next chapter explores the specifically individualized aspects of participants' religious lives, focusing on how their understanding of their practice is grounded in multiple (and sometimes conflicting) notions of the subject, and on the ways in which they subjectivize matters of belief and practice. Chapter 6 will then go on to focus in more detail on the ways in which they engage with one another, and how they create and sustain community. Crucially, I shall argue that these forms of engagement are predicated on an ideology of mutualism that itself depends on recognition of individuality, and on a framing of the groups and other structures of engagement that I have discussed in this chapter as practice communities consisting of functionally independent individuals.

5

Individuals and their practice

We have already seen how Hebden Bridge acts as a centre of attraction both for alternative forms of religion and for individualistic and politically radical thought. Chapter 4 described how participants act as individuals with a wide range of practices and beliefs, and yet engage in a landscape of centres of gravity of religious culture, through multiple practice groups. I have suggested that this provides them with an opportunity for engagement that allows them to avoid hierarchical institutional structures, and so maintain a self-understanding of their religion as both subjectivity-led and self-authorized.

This chapter focuses more squarely on individualized religious practice at an individual level. It begins by probing participants' personal attitudes towards religion before going on to look at how they frame themselves, and particularly the notions of subject that underpin this. Three notions of subject are identified, that are in some tension with one another because they posit different relationships between the subject and its outside world. Participants utilize all three in order to be able to conceive of themselves as having an authentic spiritual self, but also as being free to make rational choice and as being capable of being changed by their experiences. Their oscillation between these notions of self is enabled by an acceptance of vagueness, ambiguity and contingency, and in its turn enables a framing of the self as simultaneously spiritually authentic, learning and creative. These ways of thinking about and acting upon the self as an independent but connecting subjective entity are of significant interest in their own right. However, they are also important in providing a grounding for a shared ideology of connectivity and mutuality that underpins social significance, as discussed in Chapter 7.

Attitudes towards religion

We all know the truth. That's the thing. Because we all come from the truth, and there's nothing to be convinced of. You know, there's no need to believe in anything, or a religion.

This quote from Victor exemplifies how most participants see 'religion' as distinct from what they do. Over two thirds of interviewees either didn't mention religion in the course of their interview or mentioned it only once or twice in passing. When they did, they used it to refer not to what they themselves do, but to traditional religious institutions, doctrines and requirements of belief, seen as far removed from their own practices. Sometimes religion was used simply as shorthand for Christianity or its institutions, for past bad experiences, or for elements of practice that participants do not accept. It is perhaps significant that Victor (one of many participants who have previously spent time as members of more formal institutions) wanted to make the point that religious institutions and active professions of beliefs are not necessary. Maybe this quote (and others like it) is in part a reaction to a past experience of being required to accept specific institutional beliefs or practices. Certainly it is a statement of position, and arguably also one of belief.

Participants are clearly ambivalent about the very idea of religion. Many are keen to point out that there are numerous aspects of religions and religiosity that they like and from which they gain inspiration or stimulus. But, as in this quote from Owen, very often this comes alongside an expression of what is wrong with religion as an idea or religions as a class of thing:

> If you look at the major religions in the world . . . essentially if you do get down to the heart of any spiritual teaching, it's got that essence of good positive values that we embrace today. Like empowering people, valuing people, listening to people, compassion, love, sincerity, honesty, integrity. Those are the sort of things – good values – most religious teachings teach. . . . [However] I wouldn't call [what I do] religion. Religion for me is a dirty word. It's dogma, doctrine and fundamentalism.

This quote broadly exemplifies the main objections cited by participants to religion and religious institutions. They don't like being told what to do, they don't like being told what to believe, they don't like exclusivity and they don't like intolerance. It is notable that some former churches in the area are now repurposed for a variety of community activities (see Figure 15).

In this research, the only participants who commonly refer to what they themselves do as religion tended to be those involved with the Quaker Meeting. However, even they were keen to stipulate that (especially in the above ways) what they call religion is very different to other kinds of religion.[1]

---

[1]　Note that although participants do not for the most part tend to refer to what they do as religion, this thesis will continue to do so. The reasons for this are laid out in Chapter 3.

Figure 15 The Birchcliffe Centre. This building was an imposing Baptist chapel that closed in the 1970s. It is now owned by Pennine Heritage and contains spaces for various purposes, including a hostel, a yoga studio, a performance space and the archive of Hebden Bridge Local History Society.

Figure 15 The Birchcliffe Centre (Continued).

By contrast, participants tend to be extremely comfortable talking about 'spirit' and 'spirituality', and use this kind of language extensively. Using a terminology of spirituality carries a number of advantages, as this quote from Andy illustrates:

> I have these relationships with places – mostly they're place spirits – in country after country. I think if you go into a place with a certain state of mind, which

isn't too cluttered and is also just somehow half listening to the world, then you may make contact with those atmospheres or whatever they are. And at this point I have to say I have had visual and other sensory experiences of entities. So there's something out there.

Andy's use of terminology of spirituality allows him to talk about feelings of sensibility to or relationality with supranormal phenomena without the need for association with specific doctrines or dogmas. He goes on to suggest that he is aware of the possibility that this sense of relationship with places as if to spirits or other entities may be only imaginary, and that the phenomenon he describes may not have material reality beyond his own internal psychology. However, he nevertheless maintains that this possibility does nothing to minimize the experience as of value in its own right. The vagueness of the term 'spirit' seems useful to participants in enabling this to be talked of loosely, without the need for theological or theology-like speculation. It also allows for greater flexibility in interpreting and developing the engagement from a subjective point of view, and is suggestive of an open-ended exploratory and experimental intent (see Figure 16).

Participants use this terminology of spirituality in a wide variety of ways. As in the above example they might speak of making spiritual connections or contact (including with 'God' or other posited non-human entities, with

Figure 16 The noticeboard of Earth Spirit, a New Age shop in Hebden Bridge.

aspects of the environment, or with other humans). Alternatively they might talk about having spiritual awareness in a more generic way that speaks to a kind of broad brush sensibility. They also variously talk about (for example) spiritual experience, engagement, expression or sustenance, the existence of some kind of spiritual dimension, there being spiritual people (who have an especial interest or aptitude in relating to spirituality), things having spiritual aspects or being intensely spiritual (suggesting a heightened sense of affect) and so on.

Summarizing, participants avoidance of terminology of religion tends to reflect their avoidance of institutions that they perceive as having fixed requirements of belief and practice, or as seeking to wield unacceptable levels of control over their religious lives. Their preference for terminology of spirituality reflects a wish to feel as if they are in control of their religious lives, a prioritization of feelings of relationality and connectedness, and an open-ended, exploratory and learning-focused approach to matters of belief and practice. This suggests a framing of religion in terms of the self. The rest of this chapter explores in more detail how participants implicitly theorize their selves with respect to these three aspects of participants' individualized religious lives, and then how they understand and pursue their religious lives as ongoing learning activities.

Theorizing the self

Underpinning participants' practice is a strong sense of the importance of being in sole charge of their own religious lives. Often this sits alongside a left-libertarian political and social outlook, as in the case of Andy:

> I wouldn't worship anything. I'm also an anarchist, I have been since I was 15. I do not worship! I do not bow down! I don't see any point in worshipping it, because Paganism is also a reaction against monotheist religions. And in the general political perspective that most of my peers were coming from, we are against this kind of power over us, both in religion and in politics. Because the left was very libertarian. The hippy left was very libertarian in the seventies. So I was not prepared to substitute one God for a Goddess or for any number of, or any pantheon.

Andy rejects the idea of his religious life being subject to the authority of any other humans or human structures. But he also explicitly rejects any notion of gods or superior spiritual beings that must be worshipped or otherwise looked up to. Subservience is anathema, no matter to whom or to what. He locates this view within a tradition of left-libertarianism that he ascribes not just to himself but also to the wider culture of the hippy influx of which he was a member. This kind of view is very common among participants, and perhaps reflects the continuing influence of this kind of left-libertarian politics in the area at least since the 1970s.

A significant number of participants associate their libertarianism with a past history of feeling like outsiders and having to work out for themselves how to fit into the world. One participant put it like this:

> I'm trying to move away from strictures, and have been all my life. You know, it was like when I was caught in bed with my first girlfriend by my mum, and she was so annoyed when she found it wasn't illegal! And, then, you know we're talking 1974 or something. There was no lesbian community, there was no lesbian image, there were no lesbians on television. There was nothing. You had to make it up as you went along. So I've never been good with rulebooks and 'You will do this, and you won't do that.' I just think 'Well, what do I want?' Not in a selfish way, but what do I ethically think is the right thing to do in this situation, and me to think it out for myself. And of course I'll take ideas from other people.

This participant describes herself as growing up with no external role models or ways to understand her own sexuality beyond being presented with a societal and religious norm that it was wrong. Her implication is that having had to 'make it up as you went along' has conditioned her to be generically uncomfortable with following rules and norms, and trained her instead to think for herself and to think critically. Notably she then goes into more detail about what thinking for oneself means for her. While she sees this as unequivocally about affording herself the right to decide what is the best course of action, she claims a moral standpoint that defines this best course of action not just in terms of her own benefit but also in terms of a wider sense of ethics. Moreover she suggests that her ethical stance is developed not just as the result of her own private deliberations but also her interactions with others. In so doing she is claiming a kind of ethical and engaged libertarianism, and perhaps also seeking to distance her libertarian outlook from a possible charge of narcissism. The implicit distinction being made is between on the one hand a simple selfish obsession with oneself that thinks little about the outside world, and on the other a stance of trying to understand what one's ideal self is like in terms of its interactions and engagements with the world and then align oneself to that ideal.

While it is articulated to varying degrees and in various ways, this kind of engaged libertarian moral stance is very common among my participants.

However, as exemplified by this quote from Becks, they do not tend to perceive this as meaning they are in complete control of their religious lives:

> I've made a commitment to the journey, from my mid twenties. And it's gone in lots of different directions, and there have been lots of really challenging times and times that have been easier. But, yeah, I think it's driven by me. But then I seem to have lots of lovely things arrive in my path. I don't think I totally generated that. But I think that's more like a quantum physics thing. It's like a law of attraction.

On the one hand, in this quote and elsewhere, Becks adopts a libertarian stance similar to those of the two participants mentioned earlier. Yet at the same time she suggests that events and circumstances not in her control have had at various times both a positive and negative influence on her religious development. Her use of the word 'challenging' implies times of difficulty, but is quickly followed up with a claim that a significant amount of the things that have happened to her have been serendipitous (perhaps even synchronicitous) and that this represents a positive outside influence on her religious life. Interestingly she finishes her quote by problematizing the distinction between the effects of her own actions and the effects of the outside world on her. Arguably her mention of quantum physics is meant to imply some kind of relationship of resonance between the two, suggesting that the direction of her religious path is some kind of shared endeavour between herself and the outside world.

Implicit in of all this are (at least) three notions of the self, held by participants, that are not necessarily coterminous or even consistent with one another. First, as described above, is a notion of an active self as a kind of agency-bearing entity that has the capacity to make its own decisions, drive a person's own religious journey and decide in which direction this journey should go. This notion of self roughly corresponds to a Cartesian theory of the subject (see Chapter 3). Second is a notion of an ideal or authentic self with particular spiritual characteristics, proclivities or needs. This kind of notion of self is exemplified by these three quotes from Emma, Fran and Liam.

> I think certainly I was always very interested in finding out about witches – and I remember on my seventh birthday I decided that I must be some kind of witch because I could see the magic in everything. (Emma)

> I trust in my own inner truth these days. I did not trust in that for, until maybe when I was in my fifties. But having assimilated a lot now, I feel that I can judge from my heart whether something is true or not and whether I'm able to follow it. (Fran)

For myself there's an element of intuition. There's an element of calling. It's felt inevitable to me that I'd be on a Shamanic path, because that's just something to me that feels intrinsic to my nature. (Liam)

In Emma's account of how she first came to identify herself as a witch, she is reporting on a process of reasoning that she undertook as a child. While on the one hand she presents her realization as a kind of developmental milestone, she is also suggesting that her ability to see the magic in things has persisted all her life, and is therefore in some way fundamental to who and what she is. In identifying herself specifically as a witch on the strength of this, Emma is consciously associating herself with a notion of witch-hood which she later on develops as unusually attuned to esoteric aspects of nature, and as therefore powerful but also potentially transgressive and therefore of being subjected to oppression. It is of course impossible to know the extent to which her later life experiences have shaped her childhood memory and her perception of its place in her religious development. However, it nevertheless performs a useful function for Emma in underwriting her adult religious self-identity.

Fran talks about her authentic self in terms of having her 'own inner truth', which then acts as a touchstone for her sense of the veracity of her religious judgement. Perhaps implicit to Fran's account is a notion of an inner self that is the seat of her authentic religious knowledge, and therefore possibly also an outer self that is in more direct contact with the world and that may be more fallible. Her inner truth as she presents it is fundamentally a set of truths about herself and about what kinds of religious and other practices are appropriate to her. However, it is notable that Fran's account is slightly ambiguous as to the way that her inner truth has developed over time. One way of interpreting her account might be to suggest that she sees her inner truth as something that has always existed within her, effectively fully formed. On this interpretation, her claim would be that her life experience has improved her confidence and self-knowledge to the extent that she can better access and understand her inner truth, and so recognize what her 'inner truth' is. An alternative interpretation would be to suggest that she sees her inner truth as having developed and changed over time through her life experience, to become more fully formed and therefore more trustworthy. On this kind of interpretation, while she does think of herself as having an authentic self, it is one that has been developed over time and is therefore subject to change.

Liam's account describes his sense of vocation as a Shaman as arising from something that he sees as fundamental about who and what he is. His phrase 'intrinsic to my nature' is perhaps less suggestive of an underlying notion of an inner self and more suggestive of authentic ways of being that he can strive towards in a holistic kind of way. His use of the term 'a sense of calling' is, however, also revealing. For him to be called there must be something that is calling him. Whether that is a part of his own psyche, an external agent or simply something he invents to help him discern and understand an urge to move in a particular direction he does not say. Liam is used to techniques of Shamanic Journeying (in which trancelike or dreamlike states are used to mentally journey to meet situations and entities), and elsewhere he expresses a methodological reluctance to speculate on the material reality behind this process beyond the observation that it works for him. It is therefore perhaps reasonable to suppose that a similarly holistic view of his own being is expressed in this quote.

Many participant accounts suggest that they see themselves as having some kind of authentic or ideal self, whether this takes the form of a particular set of characteristics or intuitions, an inner self or simply a natural and appropriate way of being for them to strive to realize. While they tend to be ambiguous about the nature of their authentic self, participants are clear that it is something relatively unchanging and fundamental to who they are, that it is capable of providing them with a reliable foundation of insight or knowledge about themselves and about the appropriate way in which to direct their religious lives, and that it can be accessed through various forms of directed or contemplative practice. Notions of authentic self or of an inner self perhaps speak to theories of the subject as an assemblage, with a complexity of multiple boundaries and functionally significant constituent entities (see Chapter 2).

The third implicit notion of self is a notion of an experiencing or relational self, which is able to directly sense, connect with and be acted upon by other entities. This is the self of subjective experience and of transformational encounter. In Becks's quote, for example, she talks about a law of attraction between herself and other entities. She seems to be suggesting that there are certain entities, objects or situations with which her self has some kind of underlying mutual attraction, such that she is on some level drawn towards them, and thereby predisposed to meaningful encounter with them. Many participants talk of experiences that have been transformational for them. Here, Steve tells of a series of one-off experiences he has had over a number of years:

> End of the eighties, I seem to have got into another bad place, and my friend wanted to go to Oak Dragon Camp in Exmoor. A healing camp. And would I take her and two of her friends? And I was 'Oh yeah!' because it's really good camping. I went for the camping. And I had a very interesting time at this healing camp. You know, lots of meditation, the sorts of things you do at these

places. And at some point near the end – I didn't know this for many years later – but at some point in that thing my third eye became open. Whilst I was at the camp I wasn't aware of it. It was only when I went out of the bounds of the camp and went to Bideford or somewhere, that I went 'Fucking hell!' It was absolutely bloody amazing. It was extraordinary. I mean the first time I left the camp we went down to the local pub, [I] just had a really good time [laughs]. Had a couple of pints, loads of people, it was just a really beautiful friendly place. . . . I just assumed I got a buzz off the alcohol. But I realized something had happened, because I kept that buzz (if you like that third eye opening – there's lots of different ways of describing it) for weeks afterwards. And I came back to Hebden, and slowly that buzz went. But it changed my life around again. Within nine months I not only got a good job but I had a really good relationship going again. And I'd got a family too, which I hadn't had before. . . . And that's stayed with me ever since. But I didn't know that what had done that, if you like, [was] that physical experience, that mental [experience], of having your third eye opened – because you really do see the world in a different way.

Steve tells his experience as direct, intense, somewhat magical and ultimately transformational in its effect on him and even on the course of his life. He also talks about this experience as one that was unexpected, and he even suggests he didn't recognize it as a religious experience until sometime after the event. Looking back on it now, Steve clearly sees it as an important event in his life. It is of course tempting to wonder about the extent to which his assessment of the importance and intensity of the event have grown in successive retellings, especially after his subsequent reported life changes. There is also of course the potential for post hoc elaboration, and of later synthesis of otherwise disparate events into a single explanatory narrative. Within the logic of Steve's narrative, however, the opening of his third eye was something without direct physical correlate but that he claims gave him a powerful feeling of 'buzz' and had significant effects on his immediate feelings of wellbeing, his sense of perspective and his life fortunes.

Much of the practice of participants is geared directly towards the creation of subjective experience with the explicit intention that it should be transforming. For example, the Deep Sound Gong Baths combine an experience of being made to feel safe and cocooned with a deep sound vibration that then courses throughout your body. The overall experience is highly visceral, and those taking part choose for the duration to take a passive role, surrendering themselves to the experience that is being created for them by those running the session. Another example is that of Shamanic Journeyers who use rhythmic drumming to seek to create trancelike states in order for them to encounter spirit guides and other entities. While these entities do not necessarily have material form, they are encountered and engaged with as non-human beings, and they are able to provide both information and transformational subjective experiences within the dream environment.

While they tend to avoid making direct truth claims of the material existence of non-human spiritual entities, direct encounter with such entities is a key aspect of religious practice for a significant number of participants, especially those whose practice is nature based in its influence. An example is Hugo's story of the 'Spirit of Hebden Bridge', discussed in Chapter 5. Similarly, Andy talks about his ongoing encounters with one such entity:

> I wouldn't say I go around talking with any discrete esoteric personages, although when I'm up on Midgely Moor I speak to the Lady of the Moor because I find her helpful. And that Moor has been closely associated with her for 40 years. I address her as that. I'm not sure that there is actually a Lady of the Moor.

The Lady of the Moor is important to Andy in that the Moor is important to him and she is a way of mediating meaningful encounter with the Moor. Earlier on in this chapter we have seen how for Andy this belief in the value of such encounter works alongside a methodological openness to mundane as well as esoteric explanations for it. It's also clear that although for Andy the Lady of the Moor is human-like in some ways that allow for meaningful encounter, there are other ways in which for Andy she is not human-like. This kind of vagueness as to the reality behind and nature of encountered non-human entities is common among participants, as exemplified by these two quotes from Kate and Paavo:

> I've always felt a spiritual yearning, shall we say. For a connection with something beyond material form (Kate)

> I just felt there was something other than me. I always felt there was like a sense of the other. I've always had a sense of, um, call it God (Paavo)

In each case the vagueness as to what is sensed or sought works to the advantage of the participant concerned, not only in allowing them to avoid potentially self-contradictory explanations but also in allowing them to be open to however that which they encounter presents itself to them. They are able to encounter it and engage with it entirely on the level of their own subjective experience. This third notion of self, as liable to transformation by outside elements perhaps speaks to more relational theories of the subject, and perhaps even some form of folk version of ANT (see Chapter 2).

Summarizing, three notions of self are evident in the ways that participants talk about and conduct their religious lives. First, there is an active self that drives the spiritual journey, is able to reflect and make decisions as to which way to act, and has to develop a moral base for its actions. This notion of self is transformed by its own actions and is capable of meeting the world and acting on it of its own volition. Then there is an experiential self, which is subject to and formed by its encounters with the world. This notion of self is highly malleable, and easily transformable by outside influence. Its actions tend to be reflexive, and it can closely engage with and even perhaps merge with aspects of the outside world. Then there is an underlying authentic self, which is inner, deeper or more fundamental. This authentic self is relatively unchanging, because it constitutes an ideal version of the self, which can through various activities be sought, realized or fulfilled.

Clearly these three notions of self are not the same and are not wholly compatible. In seeking to understand and conduct their religious lives, therefore, participants perhaps shift between them, utilizing whichever one is most useful at any given time. To take this quote from Emma as an example:

> We went to the Nine Ladies stone circle. And I knew it was magic. And I think I was six then. And I went round touching each stone from the outside and then from the inside and then spiralled into the centre. And I still do that, sixty years on. It feels like it's a connection between my ancestors and my environment and therefore sacred.

When Emma tells of how she originally encountered the stone circle as a young girl, she casts the encounter as if the circle had an immediate 'magic' transformational effect on her experiencing self, almost as if the ritual of touching each stone was directly caused by the power of the stones acting on her. There is an implication that this spontaneous ritual joined her with the stones in a profound kind of connection that was not entirely of her own making, and then ultimately created a sense of connection not only with the stones but with the spirits of her ancestors. But she also perhaps talks as if there was something authentic about her inner child-self that was realized and continues to be accessible through the ritual, as if something of her fundamental underlying self is held in this connection with her ancestors. She then talks about how she has purposely chosen to maintain the ritual over the years, her active self choosing to repeat it to once again become subject to the magic of the stones and so recreate the connection with the authentic inner self of her childhood.

Knowledge, experience and belief

As touched on earlier, among the most significant aspects of individualized religion is aversion to doctrine and dogma, and to being told by others what to believe or do. While participants are not necessarily alike in the ways they think about and relate to belief, pretty universal among them is an antipathy to the idea of objective religious knowledge. For some, like Steve, religious experience is not something that most naturally lends itself to verbal expression:

> I'm not a believer in a basic way. I don't believe things. As a schoolboy I was in the choir. I was a treble. I performed twice every Sunday. I loved that. And I did get things from that. But not from, you know, reading the bible, reading the words. I tried, actually. I got nowhere with it. . . . It's experience that teaches me things. Ideas. I can't read books about spirituality. They bore me stupid. They really do. I've tried.

In part Steve is communicating that he is uninterested in engaging in verbal speculation about religious matters, and still less in reading about such things. We have already seen that Steve does in fact have religious beliefs. In his quote earlier on in this chapter he states a belief that he had a third eye experience. But what he is also expressing here is that for him meaningful religious practice is experiential in nature. Implicit in this is also an expression of subjectivity. For Steve, religious knowledge is (for example) felt and heard, and then understood on a personal subjective level. There seems no reason to deny the subjective value to him of his labelling of his past experience of transformational clarity as having had his 'third eye' opened. However, given his lack of interest in verbal speculation, it is likely that 'third eye' is simply a rough concept he has heard that broadly makes sense to him in relation to that experience, rather than an assent to an idea of the existence of a third eye as some kind of objective doctrinal claim.

Not everybody in the sample shares Steve's dislike of verbal texts. Indeed many participants are avid readers of religious texts from a wide variety of sources. Perhaps at the other end of this particular spectrum from Steve is Quinn, whose main religious-related practice is storytelling. In the quote below she talks about her attitude to religious knowledge:

> [Storytelling is] not asking me to believe in anything that isn't there, without saying 'I'm playing at believing this, because there's some truth in it.' It's a more honest thing. I don't have to say 'Jesus died and rose again'. I can say 'I'm telling that story.' And when I'm telling it I believe it so fully that I get the effect

of it without pretending that it's really true. . . . With stories I can dip in, to experience things, and then come out [and] find a safe boundary. It's a lot about boundaries. . . . I liked the Bible stories when I was little. I liked the story aspect to them, but not being asked to be a particular way or sit with a religion or a belief. . . . There are endless possibilities to find new ways of thinking in stories. To find new ways of being. There are endless stories to find and tell in a different way and bringing the present in. We don't have to read things from ancient times. We can have some of those stories. We can bring today into it, and speak.

While religious stories are clearly important to Quinn, she is keen to make clear that she denies their use as purveyors of objective religious knowledge. She objects to their use in transmitting beliefs about historical religious claims as objective facts. But she also makes an argument against using stories as illustrative examples to disseminate institutionally sanctioned interpretations as objective religious knowledge. While she does believe that stories can be used to more deeply understand truths, and for their dissemination, she presents this as a subjectivity-led activity. First, she talks about adopting a temporary stance of contingent belief in a story, in order to have the subjective experience of belief in its truth. Underlying this is a framing of belief as a feeling of open-ended or contingent assent, a standing towards an idea in a particular way, rather than as an act of actual assent that requires the idea (as far you are aware) to be objectively true. Second, she sees the interpretation of stories not as an objective process with a correct interpretation for each story, but as an expansive process whereby a story can hold and communicate multiple truths, and whereby the truths that are of value in a telling depend not just on the story but on the context and therefore on the subjective situation of the teller or listener. Third, while she values the religious stories of her Christian past, she values them as stories alongside many other stories, rather than allowing them special status. Again, which stories are most valuable to somebody at a particular time would appear to be subjective and contextual.

Clearly my participants do have religious beliefs, and indeed there are particular beliefs that are common to many or all of them. Among these are the beliefs that there is truth and/or value in the teachings of all religions, and that what works for one person may not work for another. There are also beliefs that are common to many or all who are involved with particular groups or practices. For example, all of the Shamans I have talked to have some kind of shared belief in the personhood of the River Calder, either expressed in their interviews or apparent from their practice and observed conversations. To take this particular example, the sharing of this view allowed an informal conversation that I witnessed after a Shamanic Journeying session in which journeyers discussed a potential plan for an event to honour the Calder and help to heal some of the wounds the river had sustained as a result of the industrial activity in the valley. This conversation was facilitated by a shared constellation of beliefs about the Calder's non-human personhood, the effects of industrialization on that person, the relationship of the conversation's participants to the river, and the kinds of methods of healing that would be effective and well received. These beliefs provided a language for mutual engagement. While at least contingent acceptance of these beliefs was common to those present, they were seen not as objective truths, but as commonly held subjective truths. A third person disagreeing would not have been seen as wrong, but simply as not looking at things in the same way.

The maintaining of religious ideas as subjective rather than objective beliefs naturally places religious authority at the level of the individual self. If something seems right to you, then for the purposes of your religious journey it is right. This stance of subjectivity underlies many of the specific characteristics of participants' religious lives. To take an example from Chapter 5, this is what enables Ros to feel comfortable taking on many of the ideas and practices of certain Buddhist traditions while rejecting Buddhist teachings on women that she disagrees with. It also allows for change in religious views to be seen as a natural part of one's religion, which in turn can lead to a playful and exploratory approach. Finally, it facilitates the acceptance of contradiction, vagueness and ambiguity. If there is no external authority to tell you it is wrong to hold mutually contradictory views, and to do so feels right, then this too can be accepted, at least on a contingent basis. All of these factors would appear to tend to nudge participants to take an attitude of ongoing learning and development.

Religion as learning

I have argued that participants prioritize subjectivity and subjective experience as sources of knowledge, and that this tends to fit with an attitude of ongoing learning as opposed to one of acceptance of a fixed body of knowledge. This section explores some of the common ways in which participants pursue their religious lives as activities of learning, focusing on the ways in which they frame and direct their learning activities.

The first point to note is that participants' emphasis on subjectivity often manifests itself in adoption of an attitude of experimentation, whereby participants subject themselves to subjective experiences with the specific intention of learning from them. One example is Naomi, who describes how she approached her first encounter with Quaker Meetings for Worship:

> It was experimental. I took the Quaker – you know there's a sort of thing that George Fox said: 'my faith is experimental.' Meaning we would probably be saying experiential, but I like the phrase experimental. It was an experiment to see whether, if I went and sat for an hour, I would change.

Naomi is looking back in retrospect as someone who is now heavily involved with (and to some extent committed to) the Quaker Meeting, and now links what she was doing with a notion put forward by George Fox, that locates experiment (or experience) as a source of spiritual knowledge. What she means by 'experimental' is an attitude of trying out an experience not with a specific religious aim, except to see what religious or other value can be gained from that experience, and then how she can utilize that in a way that feels appropriate and meaningful, and helpful, for her. This activity of religious experimentation is in many ways akin to scientific experimentation in the sense that participants might try something out, see how it feels or works for them, perhaps link the experience in with knowledge gained from elsewhere, and then create a personal, and individualized, body of knowledge that is ultimately subjective in nature and yet also structured and linked in to ideas from a range of sources. This kind of process is well illustrated by the following quote from Diane, in which she describes her experiments with the healing properties of plants:

> The most important thing I'd like to add is about it being based on experience rather than research. . . . I've done experience first and then researched it. I didn't want research to influence my perceptions. . . . The research was to check whether I was going up the right avenue, really. So if I felt a particular plant was really powerful at a certain time, I'd look up everything I could find about that particular thing. And so I'd think 'that's why!' You know, that's why this happened, this is when that happened, these are the medicinal properties of it, this is what it could be used for. . . . And you look up ailments. Say, if you think where do ailments come from, is it a psychological root or an environmental root, or a genetic root, you know, so you'd think about the properties in more than one way.

Diane is clear that she prioritizes experience over research, by which she means that her subjective data is her primary experimental data. In service of this, she says that with respect to a particular plant she likes to gain the experience first before researching the plant. The implication is that if she does it this way round then she reduces the chance of her subjective experience being led by what she thinks it ought to be, and maximizes the authenticity of her immediate experience. There is perhaps a slight paradox here, that with respect to a particular plant she sees an authenticity in her own experience as it appears to her, but also values the reported and accumulated experience of others in helping her to understand that experience. While she edges towards assigning the accumulated knowledge of others the status of objective knowledge, she rejects the implication that it can nullify her own experience. She looks the plant up to see why it affects her in a particular way, to validate and inform her thinking and help her develop a conceptual structure to underpin her experiences, but not to validate the experiences themselves.

This paradigm of religious experimentation is a process of finding out about one's spiritual relationships and potential spiritual relationships, the emphasis ultimately being on coming to understand the nature of one's own self. In their different ways, both Naomi and Diane are probing what experiences they will have in particular circumstances or with particular stimuli, and how these experiences affect them on a personal, spiritual level. Diane is interested in her self as an experiencing self, but is also trying to find out about her authentic self, specifically in terms of what works for her. Of course she is also interested in the properties of the particular plants in and of themselves, but her overall emphasis is on their properties with respect to her. Similarly, Naomi was interested not in the effects of the practice as an objective set of knowledge, but in the effects specifically on her, and therefore in aspects of her own self. As understood by participants, then, experimentation as a paradigm of learning is at least in part about finding out about oneself.

Related to experimentation are notions of exploration and of spiritual or religious life being on a journey or path of discovery. Tara talks about it like this:

> Stepping back from the whole thing, there's a thing for me about – I feel like life is a big journey – a big spiritual journey. But I did, when I was maybe in my late teens, go to the meditation group. And I sat in it the whole time thinking 'What am I meant to be thinking?' And waiting – 'Is something spiritual going to happen?' And nothing ever happened [laughs]. So I gave up going to particular religious or spiritual groups. I was into exploring it, but I never felt like, like anything sort of amazingly enlightening ever happened [laughs].

Tara's use of the notion of a journey contrasts her sense of spirituality with ideas of religious practice as membership of groups with expected behaviours and finite boundaries. The value of the concept for her is not so much in positing itinerary or destination, but rather in invoking openness to new experiences and so framing her spirituality as experiential and exploratory in nature. Similarly, Becks's phrase 'I seem to have lots of lovely things arrive in my path' suggests the value to her of unexpected meaningful encounter, and Cathy's talk of people 'creating their own spiritual paths' is primarily an affirmation of the individuality of religious experience, and a suggestion that each person's religious life is both unique and particular to the current make-up and situation of that person.

It is tempting to see this talk of journeys and paths as referencing the idea of 'seekership journeys' as popularized by Joseph Campbell (1993) – a work that some of my participants have indeed read. However, this framing carries connotations of the cultural itineraries of Thomas Tweed (Tweed, 2006) that envisage the religionist as a traveller within a relatively static cultural environment. However, all these quotes seem to suggest a more dynamic relationship with the individual's environment, whereby the ongoing relationship is potentially one of transformation of both the individual and their environment. This is perhaps best illustrated in Naomi's description of herself as 'a seeker after transformation, but not a seeker after anything you could say'. While Naomi does use terminology of seekership, her point is exactly to distinguish what she does from more usual ideas of seekership as some kind of quest, suggesting instead a project of change generation. At another point in her interview, when asked what she saw as being the next step in her religious life after settling into retirement, Naomi gave the following reply:

> I've no idea. No idea actually, because I haven't found it. It's likely not to be finding something. It's likely to be that I have more energy to go out for adventures in various ways. . . . Whether that will have a service element or whether it will be just, just adventuring – just challenge and adventuring, I don't know. And I don't feel it has to have a service element. I mean there is an element in which you can serve whatever you're doing. I don't feel guilty about it. What I mean is it's perfectly OK not to have some obvious thing like we've had all our life. . . . But it feels like I've run to the other aspects of myself. And that's my main task at the minute, to discover all aspects of myself. For my last however long I have. . . . So living adventurously and living richly would be my goals at the minute. But I do feel as if there might be – I might find something I thought I should do.

While Naomi is framing her religious next steps in terms of exploration, she is at the same time linking this back to finding out about her own self. Talk of adventure and seeking challenge are not just about finding new exciting and interesting things in the outside world, but very much also about finding new aspects and facets of herself. To take another example, Andy talks about the value to him of walking in the natural landscape around Hebden Bridge, and of how he uses hallucinogens as a tool to facilitate this experience:

> A key part of [my] spiritual practice is walking. And this area, and the hippie influx, has got a familiarity with hallucinogenics. Not just LSD, but of course the magic mushrooms grown locally. And I think this is a key point in the spiritual connection as well – it certainly is in mine. Because if you're using mushrooms or whatever you'll be outside, or I would be anyway. And I will be out there with a mind that is actively kind of looking. I've never taken drugs to get out of my head. It's always as an aid to perception. It's a kind of practice. So that opens you up also to atmospheres in landscape.

In Andy's account there is an element of (hallucinogen-facilitated) experimentation, and one of exploration in seeking encounter. Later in his interview he goes on to talk of the natural landscape as a 'potentially esoteric realm', some aspects of which are accessible only through 'subjective perception'. This practice is to some extent an exercise in enabling that access, and so in connecting himself with the 'atmospheres' of the landscape. A well as being experimental and exploratory, Andy's aim is also one of transformation of his self.

Self-transformation is a very common aspect of participant accounts of their religious activities. Another example is Fran's discussion of the value of her participation in various group activities, which focuses on the effects on her of the subjective experience of taking part in the groups:

> I learn a lot from them. They fill out my experience. They enable my heart to open out, and for me to feel very energetically inspired. A lot of light seems to emerge when doing Taizé practice and Sufi practice, which is very joyful and enlivening.

While Fran talks of these in terms of learning, she fills this out in terms of a number of effects on her. Some of these are about how she feels at the time of the event. She feels joyful, energetic, inspired and enlivened, and her heart is opened out. However, she also includes three phrases that suggest effects that might persist beyond the activity itself, and then perhaps accumulate over time. She talks about her experience being filled out, about light emerging for her, and (crucially) about this overall experience as comprising an ongoing act of learning. The suggestion is that she is learning on a non-verbal level, and that this learning entails an ongoing transformation of her self to become more open to the kinds of effects that she describes. She might therefore, on her account, be becoming more open to and better able to access energetic inspiration, joy and the other states that she mentions. One interpretation might be that her act of learning is an act of becoming more in touch with her real inner self. Another interpretation might be that she is learning how to be more skilled in taking part in the sessions, in order to be able to accrue more of the benefits that she describes.

Megan is more explicit about her religion as an ongoing transformation of self:

> I started teaching this Experiment with Light stuff, because it's my view that actually the inner work is the most important thing that we can do while we're here. Knowing ourselves, getting to like ourselves, getting rid of our conditioning and our negative programming. And reaching a state of joy I suppose. And I feel that the farther I've gone on with all this kind of work, the nearer that is for me. And I think there's a natural thing about getting older, you feel more comfortable with yourself, but you know I've worked hard at this. And it really pays off. Gosh it's impressive.

Megan associates her ongoing transformation with her use of (and then teaching of) the Quaker 'Experiment with Light' technique. She identifies this as 'inner work', a coming to know, in a sense becoming closer to, and thereby achieving some kind of realization of her inner, authentic self. She aligns success in this activity both with becoming more comfortable with herself and with being more joyful.

This transformation of self that is reported often involves becoming more joyful, more aware and more in touch with one's authentic self. It would be wrong to cast it as a simple transformation of the self as an isolated being, however. Instead the implication tends to be of a process of becoming more skilful in attaining these states of being as a self in the world. This is not just about causing undefined esoteric changes in the inner self. It is also about the experiencing self becoming more receptive, more open and more sensitive, and the active self becoming more adept at setting up and directing religious practice. Owen puts this well, framing his religious practice as analogous to that of a professional who accumulates knowledge, experience and skills on an ongoing basis in the service of becoming more accomplished and effective over time:

> I suppose we all take in things don't we. You know. And through our experience we interpret them, make sense of them and then store them away. And build up a personal knowledge base, and find what works for us. I suppose that's it. Something like that anyway. . . . So you know, you build up your knowledge and skills to practice as a social worker. Or any trade, or any profession. Teacher,

social worker, you know, fireman, policeman. Whatever. Bricklayer, plasterer. You build up your trade, don't you? You build up your knowledge of the work. And you practice, you know. And you improve, hopefully you know, as the longer you experience the job, the better you are. . . . As we get older we have like this knowledge base, of how we've grown up and coped with life and followed that journey which we're still on.

Religious learning, then, for these participants, is an ongoing process that involves a high degree of experimentation and exploration, finding out about oneself, aspects of the spiritual, cultural and natural world in which one exists, and most crucially the relationship between the two, as experienced subjectively. Regular practice supports this, in part by acting as a mode of exploration and experimentation, and in part by acting as a vehicle for transforming the self. What this means in effect is transforming the experiencing self to be more aware, more sensitive, transforming the active self to be more skilful, and knowledgeable, and transforming the inner self to be more accessible.

Religion as creativity

Many participants view creativity as an important aspect of their religious lives (see Figure 17), and their religious practice often has some kind of a creative element – either directly involving creative activity or being linked in some way to participants' other creative or constructive pursuits. The nature of their creative and expressive activity is as diverse as their religious practice, but creativity ultimately centres around effecting some kind of transformation in the outside world. This section briefly explores examples of five kinds of creative activity, picking out common themes and relating creativity back to the earlier discussion on learning.

Zena, a Shaman and non-aligned Buddhist, is also a frame drummer and singer in a band whose music includes strong Shamanistic elements. Although the band is focused on a cycle of rehearsal and public performances, she talks about its music not only as expressive but also as a highly spiritual activity:

Music is spiritual. I mean, now it's just my whole week. The time when we rehearse is one of the times I feel most alive, creative, engaged, connected. Just alive, basically. I'm just saying that music is this intense opportunity, that doorway into heightened consciousness and reality. I mean it's around us all the time obviously. We can experience it all the time. I'm just saying that it's like extra hype. It's just extra drive. It's bliss.

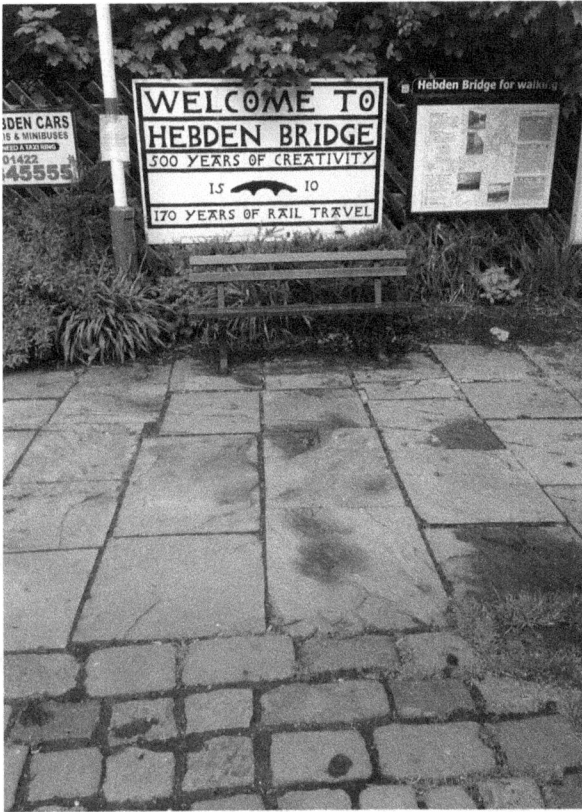

Figure 17 The signpost erected at the exit of Hebden Bridge Station in 2010 projects a town with a collective self-image as a site of creativity.

It is interesting that her description of music as spiritual revolves around the subjective feelings it causes in her. To at least some extent, her playing fits with the earlier descriptions of self-transformational practice. Yet in addition, there are elements of expression of her spirituality, and even of using public performance as a means to cause similar spiritual transformations in the audience. Zena's band explicitly uses Shamanic drumming in their set to try to create a spiritual response in the audience, with the hope ultimately of stimulating a shared religious experience. Zena's band, and specifically her own part in it, reflects a merging of personal and shared religious activity that creates connection with others, transmits spiritual ideas to others and enriches her personal religious experience.

Art can also be used as a spiritual practice in a parallel way. Here Ros talks about how her art fits into her Buddhist practice:

> When you do Buddhist art you're not trying to portray real human bodies. You're not trying to portray the contour of muscles and sinews and veins under

the skin and so on. . . . You're trying to express ideals often to do with rather abstract values. So generosity would be one ideal that Buddhist art frequently tries to portray. Generous giving, which is the hand like that [makes a hand gesture]. If a statue has a hand like that it means 'This is generosity'. So it's a very abstract concept that's being portrayed. And that's why the portrayal of the human body is very formal. It's exactly the opposite of a good portrait artist who manages to just slightly exaggerate the grotesqueries of individual human form. It's trying to portray an idealized view of the human form. And the very idealization of the form lets you know that what's being expressed is an ideal, it's an abstract concept. So I've got a photograph of a bloke giving a sandwich to a little girl, and it's a beautiful picture. A bloke gives a sandwich to a little girl. And then you've got other pictures of people rescuing dogs. This isn't a picture of someone rescuing a dog, or giving a sandwich to a little girl. It's a picture of all of the sandwiches and dog rescues and acts of kindness that have ever happened in the universe and ever will happen, distilled into an essence, which is generous giving.

Ros is keen to distance herself from Western notions of art that focus on self-expression. Her stated aim in producing Buddhist art is to create a vehicle for expression and transmission of abstract concepts, such as her example of generous giving, which is expressed in a particular hand gesture. In including this hand gesture in her art and sculptures, she is doing a number of things. First of all, she is, through the act of drawing or sculpting the gesture, performing a form of meditation on the concept of generous giving. This is an act of self-transformation. She is also, however, creating a representation of generous giving in order to transmit the idea to others and act as a base for others to meditate on. In a similar way to Zena's music, this is then a way of connecting with others, and of effecting transformation of others. By comparing her representations of this hand gesture with photographs of particular acts of generosity, she is claiming a universality to the hand gesture ('distilled into an essence'), and also therefore to her representations of it. There is an implication here that this gives those representations a potentially greater transformational power.

The above two examples focus on specifically artistic forms of creativity. In the following example Fran talks about her personal focus on being a carer and a Steiner teacher:

Where I can I will help a friend who's in need. I always like to help people who are in need. And with my own family, we've got an ill daughter-in-law, and her little boy needs quite a lot of support. So I help with the grandchildren, and I help with the nephews and nieces, and I'm there to help really. My basic thing is to help. I also am a teacher at the Steiner School, and I love all the children, and just try and accept each child for who they are. And it can be quite wearing sometimes, but each child is a wonderful unique person who needs love and respect. So try and love and respect everybody. Well I do, but sometimes I might get a bit irritated! [laughs]

Fran's discussion of her caring activities was given as a direct response to a question about how her spirituality leads to practical actions. In the sense that these are actions intending to cause transformation in the outside world, they are also a form of creativity. Her answer begins by talking about caring within her family and then widens to her work as a teacher, which she frames as a way of living out her spiritual ideas. In her actions there is also an element of transmission, in the sense that she later talks about wanting to create a good role model for her pupils, 'who shows tolerance and empathy and warmth and acceptance'. Finally, there is a suggestion at the end of the above quote that her teaching provides an opportunity for Fran to reflect on her notions of compassion and so also help to cause transformation in her self to become more effective in her practice.

An emphasis on caring, nurturing or healing as an explicit or transformational practice is a common aspect of the self-described religion of my participants. For many, this extends to wider notions of care for the environment or society. This can manifest itself in activism, as exemplified by Emma, a witch who has also been involved in various protests and other forms of activism. In this quote she explicitly connects this activism with her inner transformational practice: 'Healing. Healing is what we need to do. Healing of ourselves. Healing of society. Healing of the planet.' In a similar way to the previous examples, Emma's involvement in peace campaigns can thus be seen as creative acts that connect transformative action in the outside world with transformation of her own self, and that provide an opportunity to learn through doing.

The final example of spiritual creativity is that of home making. At some point in their interview, many participants talk in terms of either finding or creating for themselves a spiritual home. Ongoing developing and maintenance of a home space is itself a form of creative spiritual practice. Emma, in talking about her everyday Pagan practice, centres her account on her own house and garden:

I live in nature, as far as I can, wherever possible I live outdoors, and I use natural sources. I have always loved gardening, I've always foraged. I've always preserved things. My little mid-terrace house is full of wines and spirits steeping and herbs drying that I just use in everyday life. I don't use chemicals wherever possible.

> I just feel like I'm part of the natural world, and I feel much more content in
> myself for that. And I feel I really enjoy my own company – and my cat [laughs]
> – because I'm connecting with things I think are real.

In one sense, Emma is framing herself as being at home in the natural world.
Home making in this sense is a creative act of self-definition, but also one of self-
discovery. Emma's implication is that a more natural existence is a better fit for
her authentic self, and that this is something her active self has come to realize.
Her feelings of being at home in nature have thus both fed and been fed by
her Pagan identity. But at the same time Emma's account of her house suggests
an ongoing act of creation of a home environment that supports and feeds her
spiritual life.

Conclusion

Instead of basing their religion around institutional affiliation and acceptance
of prescribed structures of practice and belief, participants in this research
commonly predicate their practice on their own selves and the relationships
between themselves and the outside world. They tend to work with, and in their
discussions and actions shift between, three different implicit notions of subject.
One is a rational active self that can make, drive and direct their spiritual lives by a
process of dispassionate and rational decision making and that is not constricted
by either internal or external factors. Another is an experiential self that is subject
to and deeply affected by the influence of spiritual, visceral and other forces, and
that can engage meaningfully with other entities. Both these are conceived of as
normally in direct contact with the outside world. A third concept of self is that
of an authentic self (perhaps an inner authentic self) that is linked to a person's
fundamental nature and to their formative lives. It contains the truth of who
they really are, and is therefore relatively unchanging and relatively inaccessible.
Spiritual practice for participants is often a matter of going to as deep a level as
possible, and accessing or realizing this inner authentic self.

The importance of these different conceptions of self is that they enable
individualized practitioners to think of themselves as in command of their
religious lives yet at the same time to be both spiritually authentic and subject
to transformation through spiritual experience. Because these enable a stance of
prioritization of subjectivity, and because they are a common way of thinking
among participants, they can act as a basis for social constructivist forms of
engagement, as will be further discussed in the next chapter.

Although there are some beliefs that are common among this sample of participants, they actively dislike and separate themselves from any notions of objective belief or knowledge. However they are happy to utilize ideas and texts from a wide variety of sources, including from traditional religious institutions, to the extent that those ideas are subjectively acceptable to them. Participants are comfortable with vagueness and ambiguity in religious matters, and indeed these can help participants in their quest for understanding. Being methodologically open to new ideas, participants tend to prioritize learning as an ongoing religious activity. This tends to involve a process of experimentation, exploration and self-transformation in the service of learning how to do religion better and in the service of creating meaningful relationships with the outside world. Creativity is also an important facet of religious practice, both as a vector of learning and as a means of creating positive change in the outside world. While all of these can be and are done at a purely individual level, as will be discussed further in the next chapter they are perhaps more often done by participants in shared practice groups.

6

Individuals in community

In the previous chapter we saw how individualized practitioners can base their activity on multiple notions of their own subjectivity, and how these can form a basis for their notion of their individualized religious practice as simultaneously a project of learning, one of creativity and one of being in touch with their authentic selves. In this chapter I develop this further to show how participants in this research hold an ideology of connectivity and mutuality predicated on the notion of themselves and others as similarly subjective beings, and on notions of empathy, responsibility and the value of shared practice. I will go on to discuss how this forms the basis of practice groups that accord well with Wenger's Communities of Practice theoretical model, and how this in turn provides an environment suitable for non-hierarchical collaborative engagement and ultimately for socially significant activity. I will then go on to examine what issues of leadership and power arise in this kind of situation, and how this kind of shared practice enables transmission of religious ideas and practices.

The ideal of connectivity

Participants in this research frame themselves as individualized religious practitioners. As such, each one's implicit theory of self tends to oscillate between considering him or herself as a free agent, as subject to the effects of outside forces and as having what might be described as an authentic inner self. Perhaps in fitting with these unfixed and not wholly consistent notions of self, their framing of themselves as individuals paints themselves not as isolated beings but as seekers of meaningful connection. For example, Hugo, who describes himself as a 'free spirit in the universe', gave this as his response when asked exactly what that meant:

My father once said 'You know what? If somebody would lead me to the edge of the universe or to a marvellous mountain top or to a place which is just awe-inspiring, and I don't have anyone to share this experience with – what's the point?' And I think there's quite a lot of truth in that. So for me, well, I think there's – well, I believe in all religions. It's like love each other, help each other, give charity, do unto others what you would like to have done unto you. I mean basically it's in all of these religions. So all of these things doing, it's kind of involves sharing doesn't it, somehow. Let's say, I mean, I have bread and somebody else hasn't got, then I share the bread with somebody.

Being a fully functioning individual for Hugo is not about being somebody who is free to consider only himself, but about being somebody who is able to freely choose to share. He talks about sharing experiences, he talks about sharing bread and other material resources, and he talks about sharing an attitude of mutual empathy and love, all in answer to being asked (in effect) what it means to be an individual. Implicit in his responses is a claim that it is the sharing of any particular experience that gives it meaning. He roots this is in a call to empathetic compassion that he bases in the Golden Rule (the often quoted idea that most religions are underpinned by a moral code of do as you would be done by). However, as the following discussion argues, the prevalence of this kind of attitude among my participants is perhaps also deeply rooted in a series of assumptions based on their multiple theorizations of self.

The first of these is an idea that sharing religious practice helps improve its potency. This is an argument for sharing on grounds of mutual payback. It is based on a notion of empathetic response, whereby participants find themselves moved and influenced by the emotions and actions of those around them. This is often apparent when people talk about the value of shared practice, even when conducted in silence (e.g. as in the Quaker Meetings). As Hugo again puts it,

> I can tell you that if a big group is in silence it can be much more powerful than a small group in silence. When two or three are gathered in my name, yes, but if twenty or thirty are gathered in my name, if two or three hundred are gathered in my name, there's more power! If they have enough discipline not to chat away or do their mobile phone messaging while the silence is on – you know, common sense.

By 'power', Hugo means the emotional or spiritual influence the silence has on each of the individuals taking part, and his claim is that a shared silence will have greater effect when more people are present. This kind of claim invokes an experiential notion of the self that is subject to being deeply, if passively, influenced by the actions of those around them. He says (semi-jokingly) that this is dependent on everybody having the discipline to maintain the silence, but there is then a sense of a kind of feedback loop, such that being with more people amplifies one's experience of the silence and arguably also one's ability to contribute to the maintenance of the silence as well.

The second assumption is that connecting with others is a natural and healthy way to behave, and therefore a result of more successfully realizing one's authentic self. Becks, for example, was asked about the relationship between individual and joint religious practice:

> They reinforce one another for me. You start to see a whole change when people are in the mode of honouring themselves. They're also able to really honour someone else as well. And so you have a new basis for relationship that is not a threatening relationship. You know it's not about superiority, inferiority. It's about, OK, that person's different to me, and they might be expressing a feeling that makes me feel uncomfortable, but that's their feeling. You know, you can't take that away from them [laughs]. So rather than making you more inward and kind of narcissistic, it doesn't do that. It makes you more able to relate to people from lots of different ... and be inclusive as well, not to reject different types of people.

Becks's argument is that when someone honours their own individual religious self they become closer to their inner, authentic selves, and therefore become more able to engage with others in a way that honours them too. Of course, this answer is framed largely as an argument for the value of honouring one's own individuality rather than as an argument for engagement with others. Becks seems to be saying that you will engage with others anyway, but unless you do the individual work to get in touch with your authentic self, then this engagement with others will likely be tainted by interpersonal power struggles. Doing that individualized religious practice, on this argument, enables engagement with others to be more inclusive and more genuinely reciprocal. This exemplifies a generally held self-image involving an authentic inner self that is both inclined towards engagement with others and also able to engage well.

Finally, there is an assumption of a moral imperative of responsibility that, independent of one's own nature or the utility of doing so, engaging with others is simply the morally right thing to do (see Figure 18). As Emma puts it,

> We need to connect personally between each other for the trust to build and the love to build. .... And it's those kind of connections that need building. And that's never going to happen in the world we've got. And it's desperately needed – that's the way people need to teach and learn, it seems to me, by real sharing and real human contact.

Figure 18 Incredible Edible planter in the car park of Todmorden Station. The installation of the word 'Kindness' invokes a sense of moral imperative.

The emphasis of this quote is on the need for an improvement in the relations between humans ('real human contact'), in order to somehow solve the problems of the world. There is implicit in it an acknowledgement of imperfection and of a need to work to improve on a personal level. There is also a deliberate conflation of interpersonal engagement (including spiritual engagement) with geopolitical issues that frequently occur in the discourse of participants, and that likely connects to the ideals of the hippy era and of the Women's Movement, and specifically the notion that the personal is political. On this kind of view, the need for building connections of trust and love is ultimately, at least in part, about effecting political change. To put effort into doing so is therefore not just about proximally helping others or self-interest, but is also a political and moral choice to work towards change in the wider world. This kind of thinking invokes the notion of the active self, as it depends on assumptions of the self as a rational and independent being.

I have, slightly artificially, used the above quotes to illustrate three facets of the impulse to engage that correspond to the three notions of self that were discussed in Chapter 5. That is, to notions of an experiential self, an authentic self and an agency-bearing self. In practice, although their implicit framing of the relationship between individual practice and communal practice is rooted in these alternative notions, participants do not tend to treat them as independent arguments. Instead, they flip between these different justifications as they flip between their different notions of self. As with the three notions of self, the three arguments are not wholly consistent with one another. Yet discussions of individual and community tend to contain and segue between elements of all three, in search of an answer that makes sense to the speaker. For example, this by Irene:

> Now, because I'm old, I know that I'm not at the front line of activism as I was. That's just me. . . . But I'm asking about the suffering of the innocent. Like Aleppo . Which we know today, any pretence at ceasefire or looking after the injured and wounded is completely out the window. You know, and you say what am I supposed to do about that? How would it help them for me to be any of these things? You know what I mean? So there's always the dilemma. Do you go for your own salvation? And if you do, for me that feels a bit selfish, you see. And then people say – and you hear them say it in Hebden Bridge – you can't help other people unless you've got yourself sorted out. But I know that's not true. Not really. Because I know there are people helping each other all the time. And they're not all a hundred per cent worked out. So obviously you can visit your hang-ups and dysfunctionality onto other people if you're not self-aware. And that can be very bad. But I don't believe you have to be a hundred per cent worked out. . . . And I suppose I come from a long line of Northern women who don't think that it's about them. It's all about caring for other people. And they happen to be quite tough, so they live reasonably long, but only as a matter of genetics, not self-care.

On the one hand, Irene talks about the urge to engage with others as an empathetic response to seeing suffering, and feeling driven towards helping. This invokes an experiential notion of the self that suggests she is changed (and her likely behaviour is changed to become more selfless) by her perception of suffering in others. However, she also suggests that her authentic self (rooted in her Northern heritage) already entails a predisposition to be selfless and to engage in service of others even at the expense of her own welfare. But she also frames herself as in the process of making an active, rational choice as to how to balance individual activity in service of her own salvation and mutual, communal action alongside and for the benefit of others. While these three ways of framing her thinking about individuality and community are not incompatible, neither are they necessarily consistent with one another. Her use of all three of them alongside one another suggests an attempt to bring together disparate parts of her self to move towards an overall solution that makes sense to her. Part of the solution she is working towards would appear to be a suggestion that acting communally with others locally can help herself personally, and also then perhaps also help her find a way of contributing to the bigger geopolitical picture.

The urge to frame themselves as individuals who engage, for many participants, is then an outcome of multiple self-identified drivers that are not necessarily wholly consistent. The most prominent among these are a sense of empathy, a sense of being true to one's authentic nature and a sense of a need to make one's own rational decisions. These tend to boil down to a strongly left-libertarian perspective that values both mutuality and individual freedom. Arguably, the presence of a high number of people in Hebden Bridge and the surrounding valley with this kind of perspective has had the dual effect of attracting more people who tend towards this kind of mentality, and of further embedding it in them once they have arrived. Becks for example, talks about her arrival in the valley and why she felt so much at home:

> I loved the place. And I loved the [large number] of artists here, the creative people with alternative ideas. And so I felt it was a place where I would not be considered really odd [laughs] – which I was in most other places, whereas here I was actually quite normal [laughs]. So it feels like a kind of family. A very strong sense of community I've found here. . . . A sense of community, really, but a sense that your ideas resonate here rather than being considered a kind of complete oddball and having to struggle against the system, and what I would consider patriarchal ideas all the time. People living here (well not everyone, but a lot of people) are much more in tune with my natural way of thinking. It's easier to live here and to work here. . . . I guess there's a kind of a law of attraction [laughs].

What attracted Becks to the area was not that everybody agreed with all her views, or had the same idiosyncrasies as her, but that they were similarly idiosyncratic. She argues that therefore they were and are peculiarly accepting of diversity and of difference of thought and approach. She finds this comfortable because she feels it is an environment in which she can be different, be individualized in her thought and actions and still participate actively in community. In Chapter 5, I argued that much of the practice and communal activities of individualized practitioners in Hebden Bridge takes place in groups of varying degrees of informality. In the remainder of this chapter I will examine in more detail the nature and social structure of these groups, issues of power and leadership, and the wider social structures at play among individualized practitioners in the valley.

Practice groups

We have seen that most participants take part in shared practice groups or associations and that these can be predicated on particular religious or creative practices, or particular ends such as activist goals. Many, like this one described by Tara, are extremely loose and informal:

> With a group of friends, we got together to do music nights every so often. We haven't for a while, but over the last six or seven years we've met, and it's been quite a specific group of us – a few different people coming and going. But we're a little core and we play the guitar and sing, and whatever we feel like. And none of us are brilliant at it, but that felt like a religious or a spiritual thing that I would take part in. I really regarded that as something quite important to my wellbeing, rather than just a bit of social fun and a glass of wine. It was a really important part of me connecting with how I am. . . . And again I think about the spirituality expression, it is about the doing it with other people. I do get it out of that. I don't play much. I play the guitar a bit but I don't really play it hardly ever at home on my own. When we're together, again, because there's no judgement, there's no competition. So we sing and we harmonize and we're just 'Aaah', and we just let it go. And it's not for anyone to listen to, but it is to partake in. And there's a real – that is a very spiritual experience to have that bonding. And it – because we're not singing – well, we might be singing a song we all know, but when we start harmonising, we're just free flowing. And that is alive and present and it's not a learnt piece. And it's from the heart and it's really present. And we might not have much conversation, but if we've done that we've really connected. And that's really lovely.

The first thing to say about this group is that it is not an explicitly religious or spiritual group. Instead it is based around a specific group of people taking part in a particular practice together (that of creating music) for its own sake. Although Tara says she regards her participation in it as a spiritual experience, it is very likely that not everybody who is involved would use that kind of language. Nevertheless, it seems that the point of the events is the shared practice and the shared experience of that practice. Tara talks about the group as having a de facto core membership and then others who come and go, suggesting it has porous boundaries and a general sense of inclusiveness. There is a commonly accepted, if loose, structure for get-togethers, without any firm or hierarchical leadership (although Tara does not comment on who instituted the group or whether anyone in particular takes the lead in facilitating events). Tara especially makes a point of describing the group as non-judgemental, non-competitive. Her enthusiastic description of the act of musical harmonizing at these events arguably speaks not just to the literal act of sound creation, but to the bringing together of people in harmony.

Many of the groups people have been involved in do have a more overtly spiritual or religious orientation. Here, Andy talks about a loose and informal group that he took part in for a number of years, which revolved around Paganism-inspired nature rituals in the countryside around Hebden Bridge to mark the eight festivals of the wheel of the year:

> Sometimes only about half a dozen of us turned up, but it had rolling associations, probably about 15–16 people altogether, would come in and go out. Generally speaking we had no established practice. We set a date and a time and a place, and we'd generally meet at, say, daybreak. If we thought we needed any equipment like torches or something, we'd say 'Yeah, we'll do that', and get that together. And anybody would bring any other bits they wanted to do, and we wouldn't plan it out any more than that. We'd get together and we'd talk about how, at the site. Generally speaking, we'd make a circle, and then we'd each bring whatever we felt to it. And we regularly found that even without planning a pattern, a coherent idea would emerge from that, and we'd feel that. So we'd often also go with the angle of, say, 'let's try and focus thoughts on this particular issue', which might [for example] be low flying aircraft, as it was once. And so, yeah, so things were spontaneous.

This group shares a lot of similarities with Tara's music get-togethers. Again it had porous boundaries and a varying membership. While Andy claims there was no established practice, it seems from his account that there was among the group a common understanding and agreement of the parameters under which the rituals would operate. It does appear from Andy's description that there must have been some level of organization preceding each event, which also suggests that (however informally) there were one or more people who were particularly involved in facilitating the events. He does, however, want to stress the spontaneity of the rituals, and suggest that there was a general openness to people bringing their own items and ideas. Furthermore, it seems that what on-site planning did take place was as much of a shared activity as the ritual itself. There is perhaps a parallel between Andy's description of the shared nature of these rituals and Tara's evocation of harmony in relation to her music evenings.

A third example group is a Shamanic group of women described by Becks, which meets regularly, immediately after 'medicine walks', undertaken as individuals in the hills around Hebden Bridge with the intention of then providing a space for collaborative reflection on the walks:

> We all go on our individual medicine walks, for ourselves, but then the medicine is shared in the group. . . . We have a special process called Council. So we'll go on these walks, sometimes lasts four or five hours we'll be out there in the wilderness. We come back. You write it down. And then we use a talking stick – so you share your journey. And then there's this process called mirroring, where

the other women say 'what I heard about you on this journey is . . .'. And so through this mirroring of experience we kind of learn so much about each other. It's hard to kind of explain, but it's like you feel completely seen and understood and a sense of belonging and a sense of having a human experience rather than this just being my feelings or my experience.

The structure of this practice revolves around individually conducted medicine walks. The further act of meeting as a group to engage with one another as human peers appears to be organized in such a way as to enable an element of shared and collaborative interpretation while avoiding impinging on each member's ability to be in control of the interpretation of their own experience that they accept.

This group differs from the other two groups in some respects. It is a closed group, with a fixed membership of only four women. Informal discussion suggests they feel they have been able to get to know each other better than might have been the case in an open group, and develop a higher level of trust. The structure of the meetings is also more clearly defined and consistent, both in the overall planning and in the ways that engagement between those taking part is mediated. The 'talking stick' device is simply a small item that is passed from person to person and that carries with it the right to speak. Because whoever has the talking stick can finish what they are saying before passing it to someone else, the intention is that use of a talking stick prevents interruptions and enforces an attitude of turn taking. It is possible that the closed status of the group is what underpins the consistency of meeting structure, having enabled the members to develop an agreed view as to what the group is for and how it works.

All three of these groups are environments in which people come together to practice in a collaborative way. On the one hand it would be possible to argue that the groups have advantages for their members as individual practitioners, in terms of enabling personal religious practice, and supporting their learning. On the other hand, however, in all three cases there seems to be more to things than just that. In Tara's music group the point is not just for individual members to practice their own playing, but to create harmony, and a feeling of wellbeing that comes from that harmony. There is a purpose to the group for the group as a whole. Similarly, while learning and developing individual practice is one benefit that members of Andy's Pagan ritual group gained from their participation, the event and its spontaneous productivity were an end in their own right. Elsewhere in her interview, Becks talks about her Shamanic group not just as something that helps her personally, but as something that creates community. All these groups, in fact, are communities that facilitate the learning of individual members, and also at the same time are shared projects of learning and research into just what it is possible for the members to achieve together acting as a collaborative unit of practice. They are for the individuals but also for the community as a whole unit, as an entity in its own right.

Group environments such as these that commonly occur among my participants tend to fit well with Etienne Wenger's Communities of Practice model. They are shared environments of social practice with their own internally understood corpuses of common sense (see Wenger, 1998, 47–9), and their own shared conceptual, material and practice resources (see Wenger, 1998, 82–3). They are environments through which meaning is created, negotiated, reified and shared, and whose own existence is in dynamic relation with this ongoing process of meaning making (see Wenger, 1998, 52–5, 59). They are centres of mutual engagement, whose creative process is fed through the diversity of their members and their interactions (whether collaborative, neutral or conflictual) (see Wenger, 1998, 76–8). Their boundaries (usually porous and fuzzy) are sites of further productive connection and encounter (see Wenger, 1998, 110–18). Ultimately they are contingent but shared and mutually accountable centres of learning and creativity (see Wenger, 1998, 214–21).

This sense of multiplicity of levels of purposeful activity seems to be a common factor among the practice groups discussed in Chapter 5. These groups provide environments of common and shared practice and therefore opportunities for the development of meaning both on individual and shared levels (see Figure 19). Each tends to have a pool of ideas that have currency within the group, access to shared use of space or specific material items, and some developed processes for mutual engagement. However, because they do not tend to have requirements of exclusive affiliation or required beliefs, individuals tend to be free both to contribute in a way that makes sense to them and to take what meaning is appropriate for them.

Among these practice groups, the levels of openness and of permeability of boundaries vary from group to group. These tend to mirror the degree of trust between group members. In Becks's Shamanic group, the membership is fixed and it would be difficult for the group to accept new members. The payback for this is that the members know each other well, and have a high degree of mutual trust. Tara's music group has a core group defined at least in part by relationships of friendship. Yet it also accepts others relatively easily, and those others may or may not become part of that core through ongoing involvement. Andy's Pagan ritual group had highly porous boundaries and a rolling membership. The groups also vary in terms of their internal leadership and power structures,

Figure 19 Storytelling performance in Todmorden, which took place as part of the 'Pushing Up Daisies' Festival (see Chapter 4). An environment of shared practice with an opportunity for development of meaning.

and whether they have members who take a greater responsibility than others for facilitating their ongoing survival. These issues are discussed in more detail later on this chapter.

One final point to note is the dynamic nature and limited lifespan that practice groups such as these often display. As their memberships change, so they change, and groups (especially those that are informally constituted) often come to a natural end. Sometimes this can feel traumatic, as in this example of an activist protest group at a US military base in which Emma took part.

> Living outdoors without rules, attracts anarchists in the most positive and negative senses. It certainly attracts people who don't feel they fit in with society. And therefore doesn't make for easy communal living. . . . We started out with this as going and doing street theatre. WMD stuff. I took all these household appliances [laughs] – you know, then it was new, it was fresh, nobody had done this really, apart from at Greenham. Little bits, but we were doing this full-on theatre. And people started coming up from London and places, you know, and they brought ropes and grappling irons and yanked the gates down. . . . But then, it then set up this confrontational situation [with] the local people instead of being on their side, and help get to know them and trying to develop relationships and trust and everything. I ended up – we all ended up burnt

out. And I certainly felt very distressed for a long time after that. I was very distressed about what had happened. . . . We were actually all talking sense in a reasonable way, but coming from a different set of values. And that gets lost in the confrontation when you get any community. It grows too fast. Falls apart. Implodes, really, doesn't it?

In this account, Emma tells how the accepted parameters of practice of the protest groups changed after a substantial influx of new members. By her account the group had previously focused on a kind of non-confrontational performance protest that she was more comfortable with and that she saw as designed in part to engage the local community. However, after the new members arrived, she tells how the focus very quickly changed to a more direct and confrontational one, which made her feel distressed and burnt out, and which subsequently also led to the end of the protest and the disbandment of the group. These events could be interpreted as a failure of the group, and in some sense it would have been. However, later in her interview Emma goes on to reflect on the bigger picture surrounding these events and the demise of other groups of which she has been a member:

The image is of pools of water, or replenishment, of you know, that one dries up and you move on, it can be a hard journey but you find another one. And you share it, and then that gets polluted and you move on.

The dual image that Emma is playing with is one of groups as being pools of water (and therefore as naturally pure) and as being sites of sustenance. In likening them to pools, she is suggesting that there is only so much that can be got out of any group situation before it dries up – that is before there is no more of value to be gained. But then she also suggests that the act of sharing, or mutually partaking in the group, means that the flaws of those taking part pollute the group and also lead to its demise. However, at the same time she is suggesting that this is a natural part of the process of individual practice, which is (at least in part) in essence an ongoing process of creating and then depleting a succession of shared group engagements.

Becks makes a connected point in relation to the periodically changing membership of an astrology-related group that she facilitates:

It tends to change quite a lot. . . . It does sort of feel like I attract a certain group for a certain time, and then they've had whatever honey there is in my flower, and they go off and do their thing [laughs]. I mean one thing that happened . . . was that three of them went off and trained in different healing practices. So they kind of reached the place where they knew what they wanted to do. And so they went off and trained and now they're kind of practising that. So that to me was kind of really good. They're now sharing through their work, the same ideas. They're trying to help people coming to them to find their kind of uniqueness and stuff. So it then kind of travels on, you know. It's like a wave!

Like Emma, Becks sees each particular manifestation of her group as inherently finite, as members get what they can out of the group and then move on. Her evocative image of the group as her flower providing honey again speaks to notions of feeding and sustenance. She suggests though that the success of their membership is not to be measured in its own continuation, but in the ways that it informs and stimulates what comes after. The specific example she gives of when three women having left at once to train in different forms of healing, suggests an ongoing process of dissemination of both ideas and knowledge among the community, whereby the movement of individuals from one situation to another, or from one group to another, is stimulating to their own development, positive for the transmission of ideas and ultimately renewing for the wider community. Her wave image suggests that just as waveforms move through substrate, so ideas and practices are transmitted from one group situation to another.

Power, leadership and learning relationships

We have seen that participants commonly take left-libertarian or even anarchistic ethical standpoints, and that many have rejected institutional religious settings in part because they are uncomfortable with the hierarchical power relations that they perceive are characteristic of those institutions. It is perhaps then unsurprising that in their engagements many participants actively seek to minimize and avoid imbalances of power in their groups and engagements. One example is Liam:

> I'm very conscious of empowerment and disempowerment. When I see people seeking to take responsibility for other people's development – or to abdicate it, I sort of. . . . Certainly relationships of learning, mentorship instruction can make sense when we're empowering. [But] when they're directly prescriptive and when they create relationships of dependency or unquestioned authority, I don't see a value in being evangelical or proselytizing.

In common with many of his peers in Hebden Bridge, Liam is clearly very concerned about issues of power, and has thought about interpersonal power a great deal. In this quote he focuses on the nature of teaching relationships and the extent to which they empower or disempower those who are being taught. He suggests that taking responsibility for the development of others is ultimately disempowering for them and therefore potentially harmful. He distinguishes between learning relationships that are empowering, and those that take away power because they are prescriptive (and therefore seek to restrict the choices available to the learner), or create situations of dependency or authority where the learner does not feel willing or able to make their own decisions. He connects these relationships of disempowerment with evangelism and proselytization. On first sight this seems slightly arbitrary, but perhaps links in with the kind of discomfort with notions of objective religious knowledge discussed in Chapters 2 and 5. The suggestion seems to be that by making a claim to objective truth, evangelists attempt to force assent and therefore to disempower.

A number of participants directly link their distaste for hierarchy with their personality or anarchistic views. In these two quotes, Steve compares two different groups in which he has been involved:

> I thought [the first healing group I tried] did amazing healing but this wasn't for me. Because they did try and pull you in, just by the fact that the quality of their healing was brilliant. I mean there's no denying that. I had about three months of these massages and stuff. And it was summer and so I wasn't quite aware of being healed up. But when the following winter came and I didn't get all the pains and stuff that I'd been suffering from, I realized that it had worked. But I thought that's not for me.
>
> And that's when I went down to Medicine Wheel. And I did that for about six years. I was an apprentice for five years. Shamanic training. Because it's a wheel. It's not a hierarchy. It's a wheel. And it's all wheels within wheels. It sounds a bit clichéd, but everything's on the compass point. Say, relationships and what not. But you can say, for each part of say relationships is also another wheel. And there's all these different aspects of it. And that really suited me. I'm an anarchist, I don't believe in hierarchies at all. I'd rather be taught by a housewife from Totnes than some guy in robes, you know. And that was the joy, that it wasn't hierarchical, really. You know, you could argue back. You know, you would accept what the teacher tells you if you like, but you didn't have to dress up in all the tribal stuff – because that's not really what it's about for me. . . . I'm not good with hierarchy. I'm not good with authority. It's not because I'm rebellious, it's because I question things all the time.

He reports the first group as trying to 'pull' him in, which presumably means that he felt he was being pressured to make some kind of commitment of affiliation or membership that would have also carried additional obligation towards the group of perhaps at least some measure of conformity or obedience. It is interesting that he clearly appreciates the healing he feels he gained from his association with the group, but that nevertheless his disquiet about what he feels as pressure to accept a hierarchical relationship with the group is a more important factor in his decision to avoid further contact. He frames the second group (Medicine Wheel) as much less hierarchical, picking up on the idea of a circular structure of equals suggested by the group's name. His use of the evocative phrase 'wheels within wheels' is interesting because it suggests not just a non-hierarchical formal macro structure, but a complex set of supposedly non-hierarchical relationships interweaving at various levels. His reference to compass points suggests people facing each other as if across a wheel from points at opposite edges with equal status. Of course it is tempting to wonder whether the use of compass notions is a literal reflection of the group's practice, and if so who might have been given (for example) the North and South poles and whether holding these carried extra status in the group situation. The housewife from Totnes and the man in robes may be meant as generic types, but equally might refer to real people. His implication is that a housewife from Totnes is less likely to assume a dominant status in a group than a man who wears robes to signify his position, but there is also an implicit suggestion that the difference between these groups may boil down to differences in the facilitation style of their leaders. To examine the actual power dynamics within specific groups is a research project in its own right, but it is not insignificant that Steve identifies himself as an anarchist for whom hierarchy is unpalatable, that he identifies the second group as therefore more suited to him, and that he identifies as core to his relationship with this group a freedom to question and even reject what is being said. This speaks both to a perception on his part that some groups are less hierarchical than others, and to a will to create and participate in conditions of relative power equality.

There is no shortage of ideas as to how and when power imbalances arise. In this quote, Emma tells of the decline of a group she had been involved with:

Again it was power. It was hierarchy. It was control. . . . Along come egos. Predominantly male, I have to say. And they can't get their slice of power by having control in the straight world. They're not bright enough. They're not rich enough, whatever. And so they seize a place where everybody is saying, 'Let's talk about it'. And they talk. And they talk in a way that makes people do what they want. And it's nearly always corrupt. I find this little ABC of abuse comes from bullying comes from corruption. And that cycle goes over and over and over. And there's always somebody else that wants that power.

Emma's analysis focuses on the possibility of individuals hi-jacking group situations to feed their own psychological needs or other self-interest, through a mixture of manipulation, division, and ultimately (on some level) force. She recognizes that situations can arise that are in effect struggles for power within the group situation. Underlying her comments are an implicit gender analysis that is shared by a number of participants, suggesting that men tend to be more prone to seeking relative interpersonal power, and that links this with the historical disempowerment of women. In Chapter 5 we saw how Becks saw the disempowerment of women as a historical problem, and advocated women-only groups as a way of addressing it. She went on to say this:

> We've had this bombardment of that over the centuries, you know the witch-hunts and all of that. So it's really important for women to come into space. And I think women are naturally able to do this better, to share the space and to get into this kind of deep bonding with each other. And this starts to generate ideas, and ideas that can change society as well.

On one level, Becks is furthering her argument that there is a particular need for women to reclaim a spiritual space for themselves away from the strictures of patriarchy. But at the same time she is also arguing that women tend to have an especial ability to 'share space' in a deeply productive way. Her implication is that interpersonal struggles for power are a feature of patriarchal society and the work of women-only groups is not only to provide a nurturing space for its own members to explore their own spirituality but also to pioneer and perhaps disseminate post-patriarchal forms of spiritual association. In a place that has such a strong emphasis on women's spirituality, these are commonly held views.

To summarize, participants tend to express an antipathy to hierarchies and imbalances of power within group situations. They think of themselves as aware of power dynamics, and seek out situations that they perceive as being non-hierarchical and not disempowering of them or others. Some frame this as related to their own libertarian or anarchistic tendencies, while others relate it to gender. However, as we have seen, participants do tend to accept others as leaders and as teachers so long as they do not perceive the relationships to be unequal. This affects the ways that leadership and teacher/learner relationships tend to arise, form and develop. First, in a non-hierarchical environment, you would normally expect leadership to be equally shared. Una describes such a situation in a group that she took part in with three other women:

> We created the space. I realized that we instinctively had the rules of engagement. So complete respect, no judgement, allowing somebody to follow their own work,

but without overshadowing anyone else. It was a very non-hierarchical group. So we were all equals coming from different angles. And so we instinctively created that sort of space.

However, a number of groups do have recognizable leaders or facilitators. One example is the Taizé group, which has one person in particular who institutes the group, organizes and facilitates the sessions and leads the singing. After one session, in informal discussion I mentioned to the members of the group that I was interested in issues of power and leadership. The ensuing discussion was a light-hearted debate between the facilitator and the other members of the group about his status in the group. He insisted that he was not and did not want to be a leader, while they argued both that he was a leader and that his leadership was valued. Later, the facilitator talked to me about his role in more detail:

> I organize the venue, I do the publicity with email and Facebook, what have you. And every time I go on holiday I can't come, and I organize somebody to take over, which is brilliant. And I'm very happy. It's like children. You have children and suddenly you say 'Oh, they can walk without me!', or 'They can earn their own money – brilliant!' And so what I wanted to say is my function is trying to prevent that they go off into mind space and sort of provide a safe frame, and try to keep it on a spiritual level somehow, with the silence.

In this quote the facilitator frames his leadership role as one of provider of a service to the group rather than as one of holding a position of power. But at the same time he is positioning himself in some sense as their carer. In doing so he does admit to wielding power to some extent, in for example defining and mediating the terms of engagement in the session to provide a suitable atmosphere. It could perhaps be argued that his view of the group is somewhat patrician, but there is a sense both in his quote and in the discussion with the others that he is only able to do this under a kind of temporary authorization from them that only holds when needed by the group within the group space. Furthermore, taking a wider view, it is often the case that somebody who is a leader in one group situation will be one of the led in another such that roles will be reversed.

Leadership, then, is about power – and participants frame this as a proximal exertion of social power under the express authorization of the led, only so long as that authorization exists and for the purpose of empowering the led. One clear instance of this was Kate's description of her search for a spiritual teacher:

> Working without leadership, or some elder or facilitator is actually quite difficult. I think it can work. You know, peer-led things can work. I gained a lot from

working in the women's spirituality groups for example. [But] I felt to go any deeper, to really confront difficult issues in myself, I needed guidance. And I needed teachings, and a human teacher who would push me and shove me into areas that I wouldn't naturally have wanted to go to. So I knew that I needed that. So I began looking for a teacher. I had one teacher for while, and she took me so far, but I got to a point where she hadn't got a lot further down the path than I had. So then I needed to look for somebody else.

Kate's assessment of her search for a teacher does suggest that circumstances arose in which she felt she needed a human guide in order to go deeper and 'really confront difficult issues in myself'. She suggests that the relationship she sought was one in which the guide would have some level of relative power, to 'push me, and shove me into areas where I wouldn't naturally have wanted to go' – and presumably also then to decide when that was necessary. However underlying all this is an individualized assumption that she should be ultimately in control of the boundaries of any such relationship. She claims the power to end such a relationship when she feels it is no longer right for her, and also the power to judge whether the guide's spiritual qualities warranted the continuance of the relationship. The concrete point is that she did ultimately choose to leave this teacher and find another. Clearly it is not possible to know the full story of the ending of this teacher relationship, or how accurately the telling portrays the power relationships. However, it is of note that she frames it as a situation in which the power she ceded to this teacher remained limited by her, and in which she ended the relationship because she felt that the ceding of power was no longer providing the benefits she wanted.

Kate, like most of the participants comes across as strong and independent-minded. It seems highly plausible that for her (and for most of the others) this kind of limited delegation of power can work successfully. However, it is important to note that when power is delegated or ceded there is always the possibility of abuse of various forms. In addition, there is in any relationship a very real potential for manipulation, peer pressure and other more subtle forms of control. There is always a risk, and in one-to-one situations the risk is perhaps heightened. As evidenced (for example) by Emma's comments, participants tend to be alive to the risks – many of them because in the past they have personally been drawn into situations where others wielded undue power over them, both in traditional institutional settings and in the more alternative and individualized spiritual milieu around Hebden Bridge. One of the factors that ameliorates these risks for participants is the finite and cyclical nature of groups, coupled with their open and porous boundaries. When people become uncomfortable with any aspect of a group they will tend to stop being involved and ultimately the group will likely die, to be replaced by ones that more closely fit their ideals. Similarly, the multiplicity of relationships and group memberships that any individual has is another guard against their becoming too much under the sway of any one relationship or group.

Kate's example is also interesting because it is a clear example of a teacher–learner relationship. The common emphasis on learning discussed in Chapter 5 means that most of my participants are involved in multiple teacher–learner relationships of one sort or another, often both as teacher and as learner. As seen earlier, power remains an issue in these kinds of relationships. However, the specific issue of authority becomes especially important. We have also seen in Chapter 5 that participants reject objective notions of knowledge, take an experimental and exploratory attitude to learning and place ultimate authority with themselves. The models of teaching and learning at play reflect these emphases. Most important is a common notion that being a teacher involves making yourself and your subjective story available to the learner, who is then free to reject, accept or amend as they feel is appropriate for them as they apply to their own situation. This is well exemplified by Paavo's quote in Chapter 5. Although he widens his usage of the term 'teacher' to include reference to informal instances of learning from others, he does apply his comments in particular to formally assumed teacher–learner relationships. He sees teaching primarily in terms of a kind of act of example-setting, coupled with a sense of self-knowledge, that then provides material for him as learner to evaluate from his subjective point of view. He is clear that he does not welcome attempts on the part of teachers to find out about or tell him about himself or his own religious journey. Instead he sees the act of learning as being a learner-directed and learner-controlled process. When he talks about 'finding out who I am', he means this as active, not passive, on his part. In this way, he demarcates between what is acceptable activity of a teacher and what is not.

Becks, who herself teaches a group about Shamanism and astrology, outlines a similar kind of view:

> It's interesting being a teacher in the sense of what I'm doing, like, people can sometimes then think you're the one who knows it all. And so you have to work to get people to get to their own inner authority, rather than them projecting it onto you, you know? . . . Because as soon as you've given it to someone else, you're not feeling it yourself any more. You're wondering should I do that? Will that person approve, or not approve? And then you're kind of in a different headspace. You're back in the stress again.

Becks seems to frame her primary role as a teacher not in terms of providing truths, but as recognizing that learners are in the process of finding their own truths, and then providing tools and ideas that they may or may not choose to use. Liam, another Shamanic teacher, gives this an experiential edge:

> I've become more open to it. Certainly I was resistant to that idea initially. But it's just me holding a space. And there's teaching in terms of the technique. So I'm showing people how to do it. There's also an element of teaching that's coming naturally in the sharing and where it feels useful or appropriate, to offer my own understanding or some advice. But it's more about holding an open space.

Liam claims he was initially resistant to the idea that he is a teacher, but that he became more comfortable once he learnt to frame his teacher role as a provider of experiences and ideas, and the teacher/learner relationship as ultimately one of sharing. In the following quote, Kate, who is involved in a particular Native American-inspired Shamanic tradition, more explicitly teases out how this subjectivity-led kind of approach differs from religious teaching predicated on claims of objectivity:

> There are a quite a few differences. One is questioning. We're encouraged to always question every belief. So everything we're taught, all the Medicine Wheels and all the knowledge that's encoded in them, the idea is you take it into yourself and take it into your life and see if it works for you. And then you decide if you want to take it on for yourself. So it's not a belief system. They're tools, and ways of working. Concepts. So you explore them yourself. So it's not a belief system that you take on. Another major difference is that a very important concept that we hold is self-authority. We're all self-authorising. We're all equal in the eyes of the Great Spirit, God. We're all manifestations of the same life force energy. . . . So we're all worthy of self-respect. We're all worthy of authorising our own lives. We're all self-responsible. It's really emphasized very strongly. Self-authority. Self-responsibility. Self-accountability. These are really, really important parts of the tradition.

This quote brings together the various ways that many participants frame power, leadership and teaching relationships. Kate is explicitly distinguishing the teaching of her tradition from objective sets of beliefs, and is instead framing them as concepts that can be put before students. The job of deciding whether these are appropriate for the student to take on, and what that means in practice, is ultimately the job of the student, not the teacher. The teachings are then presented not as beliefs (note that this is repeatedly reiterated), but as tools. The group then holds, utilizes and promulgates these tools to those who find them useful.

Overall, then, these views on power and on teaching and learning represent a rhetoric of subjectivity and of self-authority which underpin and reinforce the emphasis that individualized religionists who take part in these kinds of groups and teaching situations place on these values. The focus on these two values, together with the general practice of involvement in multiple groups of practice that are loose, open, finite and dynamic, works together with and reinforces individual participants' notions of themselves as on an individualized path. However, they also provide a rich environment of collaboration predicated on the idea of individuals sharing and working together as equals. Of course the practice is likely to fall short of the rhetoric, and as suggested earlier, there are examples of abuse, bullying, manipulation and peer pressure. Future research might establish the degree to which practice matches the ideal. However, for the time being it is perhaps sufficient to note that the presence of the ideal in itself can facilitate individuals' self-perception as individualized religious practitioners who have an urge to share and collaborate.

Community

In Chapter 4 I examined Hebden Bridge and the wider Upper Calder Valley as a site of individualized religious activity, before homing in first (in Chapter 5) on some of the practices and group memberships that are common among the individualized practitioners in the area, and then (in Chapter 6) on the practitioners themselves and specifically their individualized status. This involved an examination of the different (and to some extent contradictory) ways in which they frame themselves as individuals and their religious lives. So far in this chapter I have brought the focus back up, looking first at their urge to engage and then on the ways in which they seek to relate, engage and learn collaboratively through those groups and other associations. This last section of the chapter rounds this off by taking things back up to the level of the community, examining how this picture of individualized practice and group engagement works to create a religious and creative community that is loose, diverse and informally constituted, but also at the same time surprisingly coherent and cohesive. In keeping with the themes that have so far arisen, it is a complex picture of engagement that works on multiple levels.

First, as we have seen, individual practitioners collaborate in shared practice through their membership of and engagement with (commonly) multiple practice groups of varying levels of formality. Because individuals drift in and out of groups and because the profiles of groups that individuals involve themselves in vary widely, individuals become nodes for linkage and information transfer between groups. As Fran puts it:

> There's a lot of crossover between groups. So you meet people in one group and then you find them in another group, yeah. So like permaculture, or transition town. And then you'll find them in a singing group, or a community choir. So there's lots of crossover, yeah.

It is interesting that Fran describes this crossover not just in terms of spirituality- or religion-related groups but in terms of wider cultural areas and activities such as environmental and music groups (see Figure 20). The implication is that there is not that much distinction made between groups that are spiritual and those that have more creative or political focuses. All seem to be part of a spectrum of

Figure 20 Launch of the 2017 Labour Party General Election campaign in Hebden Bridge. Many of my participants in this research have strong political leanings, towards either the Labour Party or the Greens.

group activity that characterizes local culture. The local individualized religious culture is then arguably just one facet of the wider individualized creative and activist culture of the area. As Irene suggests, however, this crossover between groups is not necessarily uniform in structure:

> Somebody said to me there's at least three parallel sort of subcultures in Hebden Bridge. And there's so many events and activities and festivals that go on. And it's not always the same people organising them all.

Unfortunately Irene did not name the three subcultures she was referring to. But her quote emphasizes not only groups as spheres of activity but a further level of subcultures based around shared interest, whose participants tend to know each other particularly well and tend to gravitate towards certain groups and activities. It seems likely that the subcultures that Irene refers to correspond to areas of mutual interest that she herself is involved in or has direct knowledge of, and that there are in fact numerous others. One example of such a subculture is perhaps the core of activities and groups centred around Shamanism, as described by Becks:

> [One particular group of which Becks is a member] brings quite a number of people doing different Shamanic and sound healing work into it. So it's quite a nice set up, because individually we can do our own thing, but we're also part of a collective where you share ideas and inspire each other. You know, you can share resources as well. So that's just one example. But I think there's a lot of cross-pollination that goes on between different groups. And I'm aware of other people doing similar things to myself. And once in a while we connect up. So it feels like I don't have to do it all, you know. Everyone's playing their role out there. And the people who are attracted to my flower will come to my flower. And the people who are attracted to their lovely flowers will go there and it'll all work out in the end. It does. It does work out.

Becks starts off by talking about one particular group as a way for different people involved in Shamanistic practice to come together to engage. She then broadens this to talk about the number of different groups involved in similar activities, suggesting a wider subculture specifically related to this field of activity. However, Becks then talks about individuals as significant nodes of activity, and finishes by bringing things back to her self and her practice, as a node of activity alongside and in cooperation rather than competition with others doing similar things to herself.

The ongoing cyclical rise and fall of practice groups also has the effect of providing individuals with a wide network of practice-related acquaintances from former groups, as described here by Diane:

Of course we've gone on our own individual journeys. . . . I can recognize people, and then I can bump into them in some place I didn't expect to find them, and then 'How are you? I haven't seen you for twenty years!' You know, and just it feels quite wonderful really. And you think 'Oh. So now, we're both doing the same thing again!' [laughs]

Emma also talks in a way that emphasizes rich and person-centred networks:

It's maybe like I'm a spider in a web and the webs all interconnect. We've all got our own. But, you know, we'll share, we'll work together, when it's useful, and we'll give each other support, but we respect each others' space. . . . There is a huge word of mouth. People know who's alright and who's not. And it was happening yesterday. You could see who was in what circuit and who connected. But it's like any sociogram, it's fragmented and multi-dimensional. And unless you're in it, you don't know it's happening. But it's there and that's the web that holds this valley together.

Emma frames herself as at the centre of her own mass of interconnections. The analogy to spider's webs is revealing, in that it implies these are interconnections that she has been responsible for weaving into being, and that they form a structure that makes each one stronger than it would be otherwise. She also envisages everyone else as similarly having their own personal structure of interconnections. She suggests that the high level of crossover between all these structures makes for something that is stronger and more powerful than the sum of its parts, and that the person-centred nature of this superstructure allows each to maintain control over their own personal space. She illustrates this all by talking about an anti-fracking support gig that she and I had both attended the day before, and suggesting that there had been a 'fragmented and multi-dimensional' but very rich set of social relations apparent. She then generalizes more widely, suggesting that this kind of highly networked social structure is strong across the Calder Valley and is at the root of what she feels gives the valley a strong, cohesive and inclusive social scene.

A number of participants cited the 2005 Boxing Day Flood (discussed in Chapter 4) as a prime example of the resilience of this underlying social structure. Becks says this:

The more people do it, the more powerful it becomes. So, it's a bit like a beehive in that all the bees are off doing their own thing, but they're all part of a hive, and maybe the Queen Bee is Mother Earth, sending out her messages of night and day, the seasons, all of that. And it's really different. And it's emerging here even more powerfully actually I'd say after the floods, with the community came together. And it's a way of, like, people working together. . . . We're creating something really special here in Hebden Bridge I feel, because it's a whole change in culture, a whole change in consciousness about that, you know. Everyone can have the space to find their unique thing, and it'll all work together perfectly.

Becks's analogy to describe the social structures around the area is similar to that of Emma, in suggesting something that is at once person-centred and part of a holistic whole. In framing individuals as bees she emphasizes their busyness – each attending to their own personal work, but somehow still being part of a harmonious whole that together works as one, and that the area as a whole – subtly framed as a non-human person – is both a centre of connection and somehow a coordinating and directing entity. She suggests that this loose but cohesive structure not only made the town well suited to respond to the floods but has itself been strengthened by that collaborative response. Becks's positive attitude to the social milieu of the area is common among participants, and this is perhaps not unexpected. For the most part they have actively chosen to live there and to stay living there, so it is not surprising that they like the way the area is. Moreover, in presenting the area as a caring and socially healthy place they are implicitly presenting themselves as such too. It is notable, however, that even the few relatively negative notes in people's discussion of the area tend not to dispute the level of social cohesion suggested by these comments, but instead suggest it can be slightly oppressive or inward looking (one person for example suggested that the area has a slight air of students on a university campus). A couple of others had stories which suggested that the word of mouth and the sense that 'people know who's alright' do not always work in everyone's favour, and that the integrated social structure perhaps has a shadow side of gossip, bitchiness and so on. The claim that this research supports is not (as some participants perhaps imply) that Hebden Bridge and the Upper Calder Valley are an unalloyed Nirvana of togetherness, but the somewhat lesser claim that individualized religious activity can indeed have social significance.

Conclusion

Although religion among my participants is individualized according to the definition set out in Chapter 1, it is clear that they are also highly social and place a high value on religious community. This is no contradiction, since their individualization is not atomized, but of the socially embedded kind identified by Matt Dawson (see Chapter 2). Moreover, their emphasis on religious community is rooted in their perception of both themselves and their peers as being centres of agency, as having an authentic self, and as having an empathic response to others. This ideal of connectivity brings with it a sense that shared practice increases potency, a notion that social engagement is a natural and authentic way to behave, and (crucially) a moral imperative of engagement.

Engagement most commonly tends to occur through informal or formal practice groups that allow for collaboration, and for the sharing of ideas, practices and resources. These tend to be open, to allow for various levels of membership, and to form as shared creative endeavours. As such, they fit well with Wenger's social constructivist Community of Practice theoretical model (as discussed in Chapter 2). Working in this way enables meaningful socially embedded activity while still allowing individuals to see themselves as, and to function as, individual centres of activity. They also enable practitioners to create their own portfolio of memberships and affiliations, under their own control. Finally, these groups act (informally) as centres of teaching and learning, of research into religious ideas, and of creativity. This creativity takes many forms including mutual acts of nurturing, collaborative artistic expression, and shared political or environmental activism.

Importantly, these practice groups tend to be limited in scope and finite in their existence. Because members feel themselves to be free to leave at will, groups die off when members either become dissatisfied or feel the need to move on to other things. A wider cultural environment exists, in which groups rise up and die off, their individuals then going on to form new groups. This cyclical nature of groups helps to regenerate and renew terms of collaboration as needed to enable individuals to participate fully and to maximize their benefits and opportunities for meaningful engagement. Moreover, relationships formed in previous groups persist, and thus the overall levels of engagement in the local community are likely increased and enriched. A cultural environment can be envisaged in which individuals are the nodes that connect groups together, and in which strong networks are formed over time. This is evident in the ways that participants talk about their various current and former groups memberships.

Issues of power and leadership are important in this context. Individuals value leadership, but only insofar as it works to empower the led. Leadership tends to be contingent, limited in scope and power, and subject to rotation between people depending on situation. The antipathy of most participants to notions of hierarchical authority, coupled with the past experiences that many have of situations in which they felt authority or power were unduly wielded over them, lead to a heightened alertness to the possibility of abuse of power.

As was suggested in Chapters 1 and 2, Steve Bruce's analysis of the requirements for social significance and onward transmission do not translate well to the individualized forms of religion seen in this research. In this context, commitment is not to any institution, or even to any one group or religious idea, but to a particular set of values, that tends to be shared not only with direct collaborators but with a wider cultural network. The particular values to which my participants are committed include ideals of subjectivity, self-authority, together with those of connectivity, empathy and mutuality. Consensus in this context does not mean assent to a set of supposedly objective religious truths, but broad and dynamic agreement both over what values are most important and what are the acceptable ways to behave (whether or not these ideals are always lived up to in practice). Cohesion does not manifest itself in the continued holding together of any one group, but in the strength and multiplicity of the networks in the wider culture and local community. Transmission does not mean evangelization of a set of objective religious truths, but a rich and vibrant environment of information flow, in which ideas, practices and concepts are continually developed, transmitted and redeployed.

Individualized religion in Hebden Bridge has social significance, religious significance and the capability to transmit itself over time. Social significance is evident in the ways that religious practice serves to bring people together, to collaborate on a range of social activities, and to create community. Along with other contiguous forms of individualized creative practice, individualized religion in this context is a key factor in maintaining and developing social cohesion, and embedding individuals within wider social networks. Moreover, it enables this to be done in ways that challenge rather than entrench extant power structures and is therefore particularly attractive to those with alternative, anarchistic or anti-patriarchal views. The routes to this rich social significance are not in spite of individualization but predicated on it. Religious significance is evident in the ways that shared practice is enabled, and in the opportunities that are created for its development, and its interpretation. Religion in this context is very far from the trivial consumerism described by Craig Martin and by Carrette and King. Finally, transmission as development and circulation of ideas is facilitated in the groups and in the wider networks, in a way that serves not to preserve objective truths, but to develop and disseminate as a shared endeavour.

7

The importance of individualized religion

This book and the research that underpins it focus on socially embedded forms of individualized religion – which is to say on religious practitioners who prioritize subjectivity with regard to religious experience and place authority at the level of the individual, and for whom this is a route not to atomization but to the development of cooperative community. It might seem at first sight as if this is an unusual niche, running counter to common-sense conceptions as to what religious individualization is like and how it looks. Indeed, the location where the research was based is not intended to be representative of the full gamut of religious activity that is individualized. However, the results indicate that some of the assumptions sometimes made about individualized religion need a further look. The question of the functional viability of individualized religion, as previously tackled by secularization theorists such as Steve Bruce, illustrates this point well. Bruce's argument against the viability of individualized religion suggests that individualized religion is structurally unsuited to having social significance or to transmitting itself over time. The grounding on which this is argued is that both individualized religion's emphasis on subjectivity and its placing of authority at the level of the individual mitigate against its ability to inspire commitment, to remain cohesive, to create consensus or to motivate evangelization. Critiques like this assume objectivist routes to social significance and transmission, such as those that have been available to traditional hierarchical institutions. This research shows that alternative routes based on the subjectivism of individualized religion are possible, and that rather than working in spite of individualization they are in fact facilitated by it. Moreover, in the particular population under study in this research, these routes do provide a highly plausible means for individualized religion to have social significance and for transmission of values, ideas and practices to occur.

Individualized religious practice in Hebden Bridge

Hebden Bridge and the Upper Calder Valley, where this research is located, is a site of significant alternative religious activity and also a site where left-libertarian political views are common. Both of these factors have longstanding roots in the history of the area, especially in the so-called hippy influx of the 1970s. Most of my participants either arrived as part of that influx or have been influenced or attracted by the local culture that it helped to create. While this is an unusual population, it does represent an example of a community with high degrees of socially embedded individualization and is therefore representative of the ways in which religious activity might be likely to develop in such conditions.

Common among my participants is an antipathy towards hierarchies of any kind, including hierarchical religious institutions. For some this is expressed specifically in terms of the institutions, dogmas and doctrines of Christianity. However, my participants generally are open to the idea that truth can be found in multiple religious contexts including Christian ones. Because of these factors, and also because of the emphasis on subjectivity, there is a general tendency to prefer the language of spirit and spirituality over that of religion. Also, very common among my participants is an emphasis on learning. This tends not to focus on searching for objective religious truths. Rather, it hinges on a subjectivized sense of exploration that seeks out and interprets experience and that also seeks out ideas that chime with that experience.

Religious practice among my participants involves both private individual aspects and shared practice conducted in numerous open practice groups. The relative amount of each varies from individual to individual, but almost all engage in shared religious activity of some sort. The profiles and combinations of belief and practice vary significantly between participants, such that each is in effect a unique case. However, many of my participants do have involvement or particular interest in one or more of the four centres of religious gravity that I studied in the area (Quakerism, non-aligned Buddhism, Neopaganism/ Shamanism and women's spirituality). Each of these is in effect an individualized religious subculture, consisting of informal and/or formal networks of likeminded individuals and their various groups and activities. I do not suggest that these four are the only individualized religious subcultures in the local area, but simply that these were the four that were common among my participants. But further, I do not think that religion-related subcultures are an isolated domain of activity. Rather, there are also numerous other contiguous and overlapping subcultures, in creative, environmental, political and even professional fields, to which many of my participants also cleave.

Underpinning participants' religious lives is a mix of different ways of thinking about themselves as individuals. These in effect represent multiple theories of the subject. On the one hand, they see themselves as drivers of their own religious journey, as able to make free and rational choice about their practice and the direction of their religious lives. But then also they see themselves as having an authentic self – perhaps an inner self or an ideal self, which they are drawn to accessing, realizing or becoming. And third, they see themselves as subject to the transforming power of outside entities, and as seeking experience that can change them for the better. These three views of the self are in some tension, since they posit alternative ways of standing in relation to the outside world. However, participants do flip fairly seamlessly between these different views of the self, and even entertain more than one at the same time. While it could be argued that this is simply a matter of inconsistency on their part, it is at the very least a constructive kind of inconsistency. Because participants do not feel they need to look for objective truth, they are comfortable with accepting the contingent nature of their subjective experience. Vagueness and ambiguity are then valuable tools. The value of shifting notions of self to participants is in enabling them to see themselves as being in command of their religious lives while being both spiritually authentic and subject to transformation through spiritual encounter.

Crucially, while participants value their own subjectivity and self-authorization, they also recognize and place value on the subjectivity and self-authorization of others. This extends both to humans and to non-human entities with whom participants (contingently) engage. It is integral to a common ideal of connectivity, which is realized in the shift between different ways of thinking about the self. Engagement tends to be seen as a moral choice, as an authentic way to behave, and as transformational through empathic connection and a notion that activity undergone together has increased potency. In members of this population, then, the urge to engage is rooted in a perception of themselves as engaging individuals within an environment populated by other engaging individual peers.

While practice groups in this context are enormously diverse in their size, activities, shared understandings and so on, they are remarkably similar in the ways that they structure themselves and the forms of engagement that they facilitate. It is also remarkable how closely these fit with Wenger's Communities of Practice model. They commonly have open membership, porous boundaries and an understanding that individuals may decide for themselves the extent of their participation in the group. It is not only seen as acceptable but desirable for members to leave, rejoin or redefine their own membership at will. These groups are negotiated enterprises, generally focused on a limited set of activities and on developing competence, but also with an ongoing internal discourse about the meaning and purpose of these activities. It is not necessary for members to have uniform views. Divergence of views can just be ignored, or alternatively acknowledged. Either way it can create space for constructive dialogue. These groups tend to be seen by their members as shared environments for mutually supportive growth activities. The range of practices, shared customs and materials in use within any group can be held as a set of resources that are mutually owned and developed by group members. Discourse about their meaning and use is not necessarily overt or even verbal, but creates a dynamic space for development of meaning as well as for its transmission and dissemination. While groups vary in the formality or informality of their constitution, most broadly have all of these features.

Summarizing, these groups provide an open set of spaces for shared practice to occur, for practice to be developed, and for knowledge and competence to be transmitted. They are dynamic entities in their own right, but they are also part of a wider cultural ecosystem, connected through crossovers in membership and through the existence of rich networks of practitioner relationships acquired through various past engagements. Groups have dynamic memberships and finite lifespans, which both act as protection against their becoming stale, or developing internal imbalances of power. Crucially, the fact that groups tend to follow these kinds of patterns of membership, practice and development is a result of their members' perceptions of themselves and their peers as engaging individuals. Put simply, these are the kinds of groups that those individuals are comfortable in joining, and each one's ongoing existence (and eventual demise) as a practice community is thus informed by the predilections, actions and decisions of its members. This kind of group format is simply the type of format that is most successful in this context.

While these groups do tend to be constituted and maintained through a sense of negotiation of their members, they are generally not leaderless. Indeed, leadership tends to be valued as a means to facilitate groups, and to drive transmission of ideas and practices. Participants who engage in leadership in various contexts are concerned to ensure that their leadership is empowering of others, and to avoid setting up internal hierarchies. The antipathy among potential group members towards subjugation to authority likely helps ensure that only potential leaders who demonstrate similar kinds of sentiment tend to be successful. In this way, the structure of leadership is maintained by the generalized consensus over what it ought to entail. Leadership tends to therefore be limited, facilitating, task-focused and shared where possible. Moreover, often the leader of one group will also be a member of other groups that are led by their group members. A number of participants either do take on or have taken on active one-to-one teacher–learner relationships, with the intention of accelerating their journey or overcoming what they see as internal barriers to progression. The power relations here can be complex, but it is evident that individuals still seek to maintain ownership over the degree to which they are subjected to the power of a teacher.

Interpersonal power and the potential for imbalances of power are also prominent considerations in the ways that individuals conduct group and other engagements. In many cases, the avoidance of institutional and external power is as much about self-preservation as it is about morality, and many participants aspire to create alternative and equitable power relations that distribute power fairly. Aspiration is of course not necessarily the same as reality, and it is clear from the data that power relations are complex and not always benign (see Chapter 6). However, the aspiration to equalize interpersonal power is a common one among participants, and it does underpin the ways in which many groups and other engagements are structured. Moreover, it is something that matters deeply to them, in part because of their own past experiences. Some theorize this in political terms (e.g. with reference to anarchistic or left-libertarian political views), and others volunteer analyses in terms of gender (e.g. through arguments about patriarchal power and a tendency of women to interact in less competitive and more nurturing ways). Further work would need to be done to explore the claimed and actual power relations in this context. However, in the light of the widespread emphasis in participant testimony on collaborative power relations and the prevalence of groups apparently constituted on this basis, there seems at least good reason to be wary of application of sociological models predicated purely on competition for domination of the social space.

Within this population of individualized religious practitioners, the ecosystem of past and present groups, teacher/learner relationships and informal contacts constitutes a rich set of overlapping networks that form the basis of a highly socially embedded local community. As mentioned earlier, groups and relationships focused on religion and spirituality are only one aspect of this ecosystem. There are also groups focused on (for example) forms of creative expression (such as art, music, storytelling and literature), activism (such as environmentalism, permaculture and political activity) or learning (such as local history). There are, furthermore, groups and activities in evidence that combine religion with one or more of these other forms of activity – religion thus often becoming intertwined with the application of purpose or meaning to expressive or activist endeavour. Religious activity therefore does not compete with these other cultural areas, but rather lies contiguously with them, with some measure of crossover and symbiosis. Crucially, individual practitioners have awareness not just of the existence of this wider community, but also of the positioning of their personal set of networks (religious and otherwise) within that community.

As discussed earlier, participants' emphasis on subjectivity feeds an ideal of connectivity because it extends not only to their own subjectivity but also to the subjectivity of others. Chapters 5 and 6 show how this appreciation of, respect for and wish to engage with other centres of subjectivity is not restricted to engagement with other individual humans, but also includes various posited or experienced non-human entities, including spirits, geographical features and aspects of participants' own psyches. This is significant because it enables participants' understanding of their self-perceived personal religious networks and landscapes to include a variety of non-human as well as human entities. This relies on an informally held personal theory of assemblages similar to the one discussed in Chapter 2.

The functional viability of individualized religion

The research reported in this book provides valuable data regarding Steve Bruce's argument about the functional viability of individualized religion (Bruce, 2011, 112–19). To recap, Bruce argued that individualization of religion mitigates against its functional viability because it impedes commitment, consensus, cohesion and the will to evangelize. While this argument is plausible when applied to specific institutions that were formerly less individualized, this research shows that it breaks down when applied to contexts in which socially embedded individualization is common. This is because in such cases subjectivity rather than objectivity underpins routes to mutual engagement and to transmission, and so those routes look significantly different.

First, among the population studied in this research, commitment to specific institutions is low. While practitioners do feel some commitment to groups in which they are currently participating, this only continues for as long as they feel that the group is compatible with their own personal agenda.

Individual emphases vary, but there is commonly a strong commitment to the wider community in which they live, and to what might be generalized as twin ideologies of individuality and mutuality. The ideology of individuality unsurprisingly involves the emphases on subjectivity and on authority placed at the level of the individual that are definitional of this research sample. It also tends to include an antipathy to traditional religious institutions and hierarchies, and a commitment to learning and creativity as subjective and self-driven enterprises. As discussed earlier, the ideology of individuality is not in conflict with the ideology of mutuality, but actually feeds it, since it evokes recognition of the value of the subjectivity of other beings, and therefore also empathy and a drive for meaningful engagement with them. Commitment to the ideology of mutuality is not commitment to any particular kind of engagement, but to engaging in ways that serve these values, and to concepts of collaborative or shared practice. Overall, commitment is not primarily to any group or affiliation, nor to the movement in name, but to the movement in terms of the ideologies in which it consists, and then to specific ideas, groups or practices as feel relevant to individual practitioners at any one time. The strength of the commitment lies not in being mobilized by any external power, but rather arises ultimately out of the prioritization of subjectivity and of self-authorization. Crucially, the level of commitment that is required in order to engage meaningfully is not set by any group or by the culture as a whole, but by the individual practitioner themselves.

Second, consensus in this population derives not from coercion or appeals to objectivity, but from multiple parallel centres of negotiation (most commonly equating to practice groups), in which meaning and practice are both constantly developed and circulated. The welcoming of diversity and the emphasis on negotiation only serve to strengthen the level of consensus about core values. Rather than a fixed consensus that is in need of enforcement, there is a dynamic consensus that develops and redevelops as a function of the multiplicity of sites of discourse and the richness of the wider cultural networks at play. Consensus about finer points of practice or belief is simply not necessary for functional engagement or transmission at this level.

Third, Bruce's argument about cohesion suggests that an absence of external authorities leads to a fragmentation of doctrines that ultimately has a trivializing effect. In the environment of continual experimentation, exploration and negotiation that is evident in this research, it is indeed possible that particular doctrinal connections may be overlooked or simplified. However, it does not follow from this that there will be a progressive weakening or trivializing of religion as Bruce suggests. Indeed, the emphasis is often on creating connections between texts and on looking for meaning in new ways. In this context of continual negotiation and development, a lack of cohesion understood as a multiplicity of diverse religious views strengthens the quality of negotiation, and is therefore not a weakness, but a strength.

Fourth and finally, transmission is not of a cohesive, supposedly objective body of religious doctrine and dogma, but concerns the continual circulation of ideas, practices, ways of thinking and forms of engagement. Particular ideas, practices and belief structures gain traction as more and more people incorporate them into their personal religion. As discussed in Chapter 5 there are a number of centres of gravity of religious thought and practice, which also effectively serve as centres of expertise in those areas. Within this environment, groups and other forms of engagement serve as laboratories, in which practice and meaning are both developed and circulated. The crossover and network connections between these different spaces provide routes to cross-fertilization and for ongoing transmission that can transcend the existence of particular groups and the presence of particular individuals. Transmission is perhaps less of a deliberate process than in some institutional settings, but occurs successfully nevertheless.

Overall, then, individualized religion in the context of this study does have social significance in the way it serves to embed individuals within the local culture and community. It acts as a vector for social interaction, promotes social cohesion within the community and inspires collaborative actions of creativity, nurturing and activism. It does all this not in spite of its individualized character, but as a direct result of the ways in which its individualized character presents itself in practice. While much further work could be done to explore the particular place of this form of religious activity in the lives of its practitioners, on the basis of this research it is evident that the personal significance of individualized religion to them is also strong. In contrast with the various claims of trivialization, it plays a rich and significant part in their lives. Finally, far from being a barrier to transmission, in this context individualized religious practice and engagement provide an open and dynamic environment in which ideas, practices and concepts can be and are continually developed, refined and circulated.

Caveats

The question that this research set out to address concerned the capability for structural viability of individualized religion. The aim was therefore to explore a particular context in which individualized religion is clearly prevalent, and especially the extent to which individualized religion in this context has the capability for social significance and the capability to transmit itself over time. Unsurprisingly, my conclusion that it does is closely related to my conclusions about the form in which individualized religion takes in this particular context. In drawing wider conclusions there are a number of caveats that should be borne in mind.

The first caveat relates to the use of participant testimony as a key source of evidence. The methodology of this research focused on a kind of triangulation between how participants spoke about their religious practices and engagements, observation of these engagements in practice and ongoing assessment on my part as to the reliability and believability of participant accounts. It could be argued that I have given too much emphasis to the expressed attitudes and self-assessments of participants, and therefore given too much credence to the ways they wanted to present themselves and be perceived. In response to this I would argue that the triangulation mentioned earlier has helped to guard against grossly dissembling or self-serving accounts. But in addition, the ways in which participants want to be perceived is valuable data in itself, insofar as it is a key ground on which they come together with others to form groups. If participants were to seek to come across to me vastly differently to how they seek to come across to their peers, there would likely have been some indication of this in my observations of intra-group engagements. If they were to dishonestly present themselves both to me and to their group peers as holding a particular value, then this would not negate my observations that those peer engagements are predicated on the mutual expression of that value.

A second caveat regards potential differences between different forms of individualized religion. A deliberate decision was made not to divide the participants according to the content of their religious practice, but instead to treat individualized practitioners as a class irrespective of their specific religious beliefs and practices. Four centres of gravity were observed within this population (Quakerism, non-aligned Buddhism, Neopagan and Shamanistic practices, and women's spirituality). While this methodology did enable common patterns to be observed across the wider class of individualized practitioners, it could be argued that it would have failed to pick up on differences between those involved in each of these four centres of gravity (or indeed others that may exist). The methodology as undertaken can be defended on the grounds that in practice the boundaries between these centres of gravity are extremely diffuse and fuzzy, and that what is of real interest are the patterns, practices and ideologies that span the different religious centres of gravity. However, the trade-off is that limited information was gained regarding the relation between religious content and religious structure, or regarding differences in structural viability between these centres of gravity.

My third caveat concerns what wider conclusions can be drawn from this research. While the research has provided evidence and theoretical justification for the existence of potential routes to social and religious significance and to ongoing transmission, further work could be done to explore how these routes play out in practice, and develop over time. A particular issue is that this research focused largely on members of a single generation, and was of short duration. It would be useful for further study to follow how the relationships between individuals, groups and cultures develop over time and over generations, and to delve deeper into the extent and breadth of social connections, and the particular power relations at play.

The final caveat concerns generalizability. The starting off point was an argument that theoretical models previously applied to individualized religion to argue for its structural weakness are inappropriate, because they are predicated on the structures and assumptions of hierarchical religious institutions. This research has provided evidence that social significance, religious significance and transmission are observable in one small population of individualized practitioners, and that in this particular context individualized religion is therefore not structurally weak in the way previously claimed. I have further gone on to argue that its structural viability in this context, rather than being in spite of its individualized character, is rooted firmly within it. However, the extent to which this argument is generalizable to other contexts remains to be demonstrated. My initial theorization is based on a distinction between disembedded individualization and embedded individualization, arguing only that the latter is potentially structurally viable. Hebden Bridge and its surrounding is arguably an unusual social context, due to its somewhat enclosed geographical situation and its history as a site of non-conformist and then alternative religion. It is perhaps therefore an environment in which a greater degree of embedded individualization persists than elsewhere. If individualized religious practitioners elsewhere are more disembedded and atomized, then the claims made against its structural viability in those contexts may well still hold. There is a further story to be told about whether practitioners who are in communities in which individualized religion is less prominent are able to find opportunities to engage in the ways that are prevalent in Hebden Bridge.

The value of this research

Despite the above caveats, this research shows that individualized religion is functionally viable – that is, that it has the potential to have social significance and to transmit itself over time. This provides a source of challenge for the arguments of secularization theorists that individualization is a purely secularizing phenomenon. Perhaps more importantly, this research has provided a theoretical basis with which to understand and model how individualized practice can embed individuals in community, be a source of socially significant interactions and activities, and transmit itself over time. While this does not directly address the argument that individualized religion has been part of the story of secularization in Britain, it adds significant nuance to ongoing discussions about the place of individualized religion in this secularized society. This work builds on and brings together the work of various authors, notably Matt Dawson's analysis of critiques of individualization (Dawson, 2012), Gilles Deleuze and Félix Guattari's concept of assemblages (Deleuze and Guattari, 2013) and Etienne Wenger's popularization and explication of the Communities of Practice model (Wenger, 1998). In so doing, it also provides an account of what characteristics of individual practice and engagement are likely to be indicators of socially or religiously significant individualized religious practice.

The distinction between disembedded (or atomized) forms of individualization and socially embedded forms is crucial, since it cuts through a commonly held perception that there is a fundamental opposition between individual and community (and therefore also society). The theoretical analyses in this thesis explore how social engagement is able not merely to coexist with individualization, but actually be predicated on it. That is, it allows for mutuality and community to arise from the understanding of practitioners of themselves as self-authorizing, and from their perceptions that this brings with it recognition of the parallel status of others, and both a desire and a duty to be in meaningful community with other individuals on terms of equality. The use of the concept of assemblages allows for individuals to be given functional equivalence not only to their peers but also to non-human entities, and to groups or structures with which they engage. This also provides a theoretical structure to aid in understanding the ways in which individualized practitioners in this context view themselves in the world and view their engagements as radically horizontal.

The application of the Communities of Practice model to the groups and other engagements in which these individualized practitioners involve themselves was in effect the testing of a hypothesis that these groups could be well described by the elements of that model. The evidence of this research is that this is the case. Arguably this is an unsurprising conclusion, since the model was originally based on an assumption that humans are social and explorative in nature, and a claim that groups such as these can therefore spontaneously arise in various contexts (Wenger, 1998, 2, 7). However, the value of the application of this model in Chapter 6 alongside the analysis of individual practitioners' religious lives in Chapter 5 is that it provides a coherent explanation of how it is possible for mutuality and subjectivity to take the place of hierarchy and objectivity in sustaining religious community. This kind of analysis is of course potentially extendible to other contexts of alternative and non-hierarchical religious engagement, to vernacular religion, and even to the engagements that go on in practice alongside the formally constituted power structures of traditional religious institutions. Studying engagement as spontaneous and informal practice communities could also be a potential way of exploring the crossover between religion and various creative or activist subcultures. Also of value in this research is the linkage made between engagements through these informal groups and the wider networks of contacts and associations around each individual, and the way these can serve to maintain a dynamic and cohesive culture and local community in the absence of hierarchical institutions and objectivist assumptions. These considerations could potentially be applied more widely.

Another area of value arising from this research is in study of the creation, circulation and transmission of knowledge in religious contexts (and especially in alternative religious or vernacular religious contexts). Because practice communities provide a space in which meaning can be negotiated and shared, they – together with the wider community networks – can potentially form a basis for dynamic and meaningful religious activity in the absence of hierarchies and institutions. The application of this model potentially provides a way to understand and chart the development, circulation and transmission of practices and ideas.

Finally, this research picks up on and brings together concerns about traditional sociological analyses of engagement as involving struggles for domination of the social space. There is here a confluence between the importance that participants claim to place on cooperative and equitable interpersonal power relations, and the aim of the Communities of Practice model to go beyond conflictual or over-simplified theorizations (Wenger, 1998, 15). While the expressed aim of participants is of importance in that it speaks to a commonly shared ideal of cooperation, study of particular groups using the Communities of Practice model can potentially serve to nuance and complexify the ways that interpersonal power in these kinds of contexts are visualized and understood.

Looking forward

This research has potentially significant implications for the ongoing discussions about secularization, about the various changes that are occurring in the religious landscape and especially about the religious status of those who are outside of traditional religious institutions. It provides a clear challenge to arguments that privatization and individualization are necessarily secularizing phenomena. It therefore supports those authors who have argued for the significance and importance of alternative, non-institutional and non-traditional religious forms. Specifically, it not only supports the idea of a growing and increasingly significant subjective turn, as, for example, advocated by Paul Heelas and Linda Woodhead (Heelas and Woodhead, 2005), but goes further in showing how religion outside of traditional institutional contexts can be transmitted from person to person, and also (theoretically) through time. In addition it provides tools for the further explication of specific alternative (and other) religious contexts, by facilitating the theoretical treatment of socially significant engagement without requirement for direct correlates of institutions, hierarchies and dogmas. In positing potential routes for ongoing transmission of alternative and non-institutional religious ideas and praxis, this research adds a fresh perspective to work such as that of Marion Bowman that indicates persistence of religious influence in individualized contexts transcending the presence of particular individuals or groups (Bowman, 2009, 165–8). This research also provides both support and explanatory tools for the ongoing live fields of study into vernacular religion (Bowman and Valk, 2012b), and the so-called religious 'nones' (those who claim on surveys to be nonreligious; Lee, 2012, 139).

In addition, this research has implications for a variety of approaches and potential approaches to the religious individual. Specifically, it shows that how the individual frames themself and their subjectivity can be a crucial component in how religious community forms, develops and persists. It also then provides a range of methodological and theological tools with which to approach the individual understood in this way. This approach, influenced as it is by postmodernism and social constructivism, problematizes both disembedded concepts of individualism and also notions of consumer religion, since it invites researchers to understand individualized practitioners not just as choosers or consumers, but as active and engaged producers of religious content and praxis. It also invites academics to take seriously the idea of the individual as a constructive interlocutor, not only with their human peers but with a variety of non-human persons. In so doing, it provides particular conceptual tools for study of animism and related world views (see Harvey, 2005).

However, this research also has implications beyond religion. It is located within a much bigger set of debates about what kind of society we are living in, and in which direction our society is heading. It problematizes the commonly held view that it is only formalized hierarchical institutions that can embed individuals into society. It instead demonstrates that informal structures of engagement can be highly effective vectors for the building and maintaining of the social embeddedness of individuals. In an age of increasingly digital and grassroots-led politics and of growing populism, this supports Manuel Castells' notion of the emergence of networked social movements as not only a powerful social force but as one that is non-hierarchical, non-programmatic, and potentially highly creative (Castells, 2012, 221–37).

Perhaps most significantly, this research has implications on our understanding of the way that interpersonal power relations play out in the context of informal groups and networks. It indicates that both cooperation over the wielding of interpersonal power and rejection of contexts of power imbalance can be significant factors in the development and maintenance of informal social organization. Most particularly, this problematizes commonly held assumptions that social engagement is ultimately predicated on an ongoing struggle for domination of the social space (e.g. see Bourdieu, 1977, 11–15). Instead, this research invites us to take seriously charges that this constitutes a gendered view of capital that perpetuates sexist dichotomies, and consequent calls for the recognition and development of feminist conceptualizations of habitus (McCall, 1992).

For all of these reasons, it is of paramount importance to undertake more research to understand the nature of the various non-formal structures of engagement that are predicated on and that facilitate individuals working together for material social change – from religious practice groups to the wider cultural networks in which they exist. At a time when the direction of society is being increasingly influenced (and indeed fought over) by movements that grow from the bottom up through social media and other non-formal structures, there is a pressing need to better understand the means by which individuals create, modulate and recreate spaces of shared values and shared creativity. Most specifically, we need to avoid the all too common assumptions that in such spaces the majority of participants are merely being manipulated, dominated or acting through herd mentality. Instead we should entertain the possibility that underwriting such movements might be effective informally constituted structures of engagement, which are allowing individuals to share, negotiate and develop their values and then to use these as a base for mutualized and shared action. Such research would be important to conduct at any time, but perhaps most especially now.

Conclusion

The ethnographic study on which this book is based focused on the forms of association and transmission among non-institutional and semi-institutional religious practitioners in and around Hebden Bridge. The character and form of the religion of the participants in this study are informed by the social history of the area, and particularly the counterculture of the 1970s. The subjects of the research are not only individualized but invested in their individualized status. They prioritize subjectivity and they understand themselves as their primary sources of religious authority. Their religion tends to be explorative in nature. They are involved in a wide and diverse variety of religious practices, and are very suspicious of religious institutions, hierarchies, rules and dogmas. They participate together actively in an overlapping and cross-linking informal network of loose practice communities and other informal associations, that tend to exhibit the elements of Wenger's Community of Practice model. These groups act as spaces in which participants practice together, and in which they develop and circulate ideas. These engagements propagate and sustain core ideologies of individualization, connectivity and mutualization, and act as vehicles for socially and religiously significant activity that is ultimately predicated on individuals' various notions of individuality. They also enable an ongoing and dynamic flow of ideas, interpretations and practices to occur.

In this context religious activity is just one aspect of a wider sphere of activity that also includes arenas of artistic creativity, experiments in alternative living and environmental and political activism. While propagation and dissemination in this milieu do not occur in the same way as in institutional or hierarchical settings, the evidence shows that the combination of informal structures and practices at play does provide a potentially viable basis for socially significant religious activity and for its ongoing propagation over time. Moreover, this research, and the model of individualized religion that it has developed, has potentially significant implications for the broader study of the ways in which individualized and non-formal engagement can enable individuals to come together as individuals to form active and engaged social movements.

Bibliography

Barker, P. (2012a). *Hebden Bridge: A Sense of Belonging*, London: Frances Lincoln.

Barker, P. (2012b). 'Hebden Bridge: West Yorkshire's cool and quirky corner', *The Guardian (online version)*, 4 May 2012 [Online]. Accessed at http://www.theguardian.com/travel/2012/may/04/hebden-bridge-cultural-centre-yorkshire (Accessed 28 January 2019).

Baumann, Z. (1992). *Intimations of Postmodernity*, Oxford: Routledge.

Bennett, J. (2010). *Vibrant Matter: A Political Ecology of Things*, Durham, NC: Duke University Press.

Berger, P. (2012). *The Sacred Canopy: Elements of a Sociological Theory*, New York: Open Road.

Berger, P. (2014). *The Many Altars of Modernity: Toward a Paradigm of Religion in a Pluralist Age*, Boston: de Gruyter.

Binns, A. (2013). *Valley of a Hundred Chapels: Yorkshire Non-Conformists' Lives and Legacies*, Heptonstall: Grace Judson Press.

Bollier, D. (2013). *Silent Theft: The Private Plunder of Our Common Wealth*, London: Routledge.

Bourdieu, P. (1977). *Outline of a Theory of Practice*, Cambridge: Cambridge University Press.

Bowman, M. (1999). 'Healing in the spiritual marketplace: Consumers, courses and credentialism', *Social Compass*, vol. 46, no. 2, pp. 181–9.

Bowman, M. (2009). 'Learning from experience: The value of analysing Avalon', *Religion*, vol. 39, no. 2, pp. 161–8.

Bowman, M. (2013). 'Valuing spirituality: Commodification, consumption and community in Glastonbury', in F. Gauthier and T. Martikainen (eds), *Religion in Consumer Society: Brands, Consumers and Markets*, Farnham: Ashgate, pp. 207–24.

Bowman, M. (2016). '"Helping Glastonbury come into its own": Practical spirituality, materiality, and community cohesion in Glastonbury', in C. Coats and M. Emerich (eds), *Practical Spiritualities in a Media Age*, London: Bloomsbury, pp. 51–66.

Bowman, M. and Valk, Ü. (2012). 'Introduction: Vernacular religion, generic expressions and the dynamics of belief', in M. Bowman and Ü. Valk (eds), *Vernacular Religion in Everyday Life*, Sheffield: Equinox, pp. 1–19.

Boyne, R. (2001). *Subject, Society and Culture*, London: Sage.

Brown, C. (2009). *The Death of Christian Britain: Understanding Secularisation 1800–2000*, Abingdon: Routledge.

Bruce, S. (1996). *Religions in the Modern World: From Cathedrals to Cults*, Oxford: Oxford University Press.

Bruce, S. (2001). 'The curious case of the unnecessary recantation: Berger and secularization', in L. Woodhead, P. Heelas and D. Martin (eds), *Peter Berger and the Study of Religion*, Abingdon: Routledge, pp. 87–100.

Bruce, S. (2003). 'The demise of Christianity in Britain', in G. Davie, P. Heelas and L. Woodhead (eds), *Predicting Religion: Christian, Secular and Alternative Futures*, Aldershot: Ashgate, pp. 53–63.

Bruce, S. (2006). 'Secularization and the impotence of individualized religion', *The Hedgehog Review*, vol. 8, no. 1–2, pp. 35–45.

Bruce, S. (2011). *Secularization: In Defence of an Unfashionable Theory*, Oxford: Oxford University Press.

Bruce, S. and Voas, D. (2007). 'Religious toleration and organisational typologies', *Journal of Contemporary Religion*, vol. 22, no. 1, pp. 1–17.

Buber, M. (2004). *I and Thou*, London: Continuum.

Campbell, J. (1993). *The Hero with a Thousand Faces*, London: Fontana.

Carrette, J. and King, R. (2005). *Selling Spirituality: The Silent Takeover of Religion*, Abingdon: Routledge.

Casanova, J. (2006). 'Rethinking secularization: A global comparative perspective', *The Hedgehog Review*, vol. 8, no. 1–2, pp. 7–22.

Casanova, J. (2011). 'The secular, secularizations and secularisms', in C. Calhoun, M. Jeurgensmeyer and J. Van Antwerpen (eds), *Rethinking Secularism*, Oxford: Oxford University Press, pp. 54–74.

Castells, M. (2000). *The Rise of the Network Society*, Oxford: Blackwell.

Castells, M. (2012). *Networks of Outrage and Hope: Social Movements in the Digital Age*, Cambridge: Polity Press.

CoolPlaces. (2015). *Hebden Bridge* [online]. Available at: http://www.coolplaces.co.uk/guides/uk/england/yorkshire/97-hebden-bridge (Accessed 28 January 2019).

Corrywright, D. (2003). *Theoretical and Empirical Investigations into New Age Spiritualities*, Bern: Peter Lang.

Davie, G. (1994). *Religion in Britain Since 1945: Believing Without Belonging*, Oxford: Blackwell.

Davie, G. (2006). 'Religion in Europe in the 21st Century: The factors to take into account', *European Journal of Sociology / Archives Européennes de Sociologie*, vol. 47, no. 2, pp. 271–96.

Davie, G. (2015). *Religion in Britain: A Persistent Paradox*, Chichester: John Wiley.

Dawson, A. (2011). 'Consuming the self: New spirituality as "mystified consumption"', *Social Compass*, vol. 58, no. 3, pp. 309–15.

Dawson, M. (2012). 'Reviewing the critique of individualization: The disembedded and embedded theses', *Acta Sociologica*, vol. 55, no. 4, pp. 305–19.

Deleuze, G. and Guattari, F. (2013). *A Thousand Plateaus*, London: Bloomsbury Academic.

Descartes, R. (1968). *Discourse on Method and the Meditations*, London: Penguin.

Dobbelaere, K. (2002). *Secularization: An Analysis at Three Levels*, Brussels: Peter Lang.

Dobbelaere, K. (2007). 'Testing secularization theory in comparative perspective', *Nordic Journal of Religion and Society*, vol. 20, no. 2, pp. 137–47.

Dobbelaere, K. (2014). 'The Karel Dobbelaere lecture: From the study of religions to the study of meaning systems', *Social Compass*, vol. 61, no. 2, pp. 219–33.

Durkheim, E. (1951). *Suicide: A Sociological Study*, Abingdon: Routledge.

Durkheim, E. (2001). *The Elementary Forms of Religious Life*, Oxford: Oxford University Press.

Durkheim, E. (2014). *The Division of Labor in Society*, New York: Free Press.

Gauthier, F., Woodhead, L. and Martikainen, T. (2013). 'Introduction: Consumerism as the ethos of consumer society', in F. Gauthier and T. Martikainen (eds), *Religion in Consumer Society: Brands, Consumers and Markets*, Farnham: Ashgate, pp. 1–26.

Gilhus, I. S. (2012). 'Angels in Norway: Border-crossers and border-markers', in M. Bowman and Ü. Valk (eds), *Vernacular Religion in Everyday Life: Expressions of Belief*, Sheffield: Equinox, pp. 230–45.

González, G. (2015). 'The ritualization of consumer capitalism: Catherine Bell's Ritual Theory, ritual practice in the age of Starbucks', *Implicit Religion*, vol. 18, no. 1, pp. 3–44.

Haraway, D. (1988). 'Situated knowledges: The science question in feminism and the privilege of partial perspective', *Feminist Studies*, vol. 14, no. 3, pp. 575–99.

Harvey, G. (2005). *Animism: Respecting the Living World*, London: Hurst & Company.

Harvey, G. and Vincett, G. (2012). 'Alternative spiritualities: Marginal and mainstream', in L. Woodhead and R. Catto (eds), *Religion and Change in Modern Britain*, Abingdon: Routledge, pp. 156–72.

HBLHS. (2017). *How the Hippies Changed Hebden Bridge* [online]. Available at: http://www.hebdenbridge.co.uk/hippies/pdfs/Hebden-Bridge-Hippies.pdf (Accessed 28 January 2019).

HBW. (2005). *Hebden Bridge: 4th Funkiest Town in the World* [online]. Available at: http://www.hebdenbridge.co.uk/news/news05/17.html (Accessed 28 January 2019).

HBW. (2016). *Hebden Bridge Web* [online]. Available at: http://www.hebdenbridge.co.uk/index.html (Accessed 28 January 2019).

Heelas, P. (1996). *The New Age Movement: The Celebration of the Self and the Sacralisation of Modernity*, Oxford: Blackwell.

Heelas, P. and Woodhead, L. (2005). *The Spiritual Revolution: Why Religion Is Giving Way to Spirituality*, Oxford: Blackwell.

Heidegger, M. (2000). *Being and Time*, Oxford: Blackwell.

Holloway, J. (2000). 'Institutional geographies of the New Age movement', *Geoforum*, vol. 31, no. 4, pp. 553–65.

Jennings, B. (1992). *Pennine Valley: A History of Upper Calderdale* – Hebden Bridge WEA Local History Group, Hebden Bridge: Hebden Bridge Local History Society.

Lassander, M. (2012). 'Grappling with liquid modernity: Investigating post-secular religion', in P. Nynäs, M. Lassander and T. Utriainen (eds), *Post-Secular Society*, Piscataway: Transaction Publishers, pp. 239–68.

Latour, B. (2005). *Reassembling the Social: An Introduction to Actor-Network Theory*, Oxford: Oxford University Press.

Lee, L. (2012). 'Locating nonreligion, in mind, body and space: New research methods for a new field', *Annual Review of the Sociology of Religion [Online]*, vol. 3, pp. 135–7.

Leidner, D. E. and Jarvenpaa, S. L. (1995). 'The use of information technology to enhance management school education: A theoretical view', *MIS Quarterly*, vol. 19, no. 3, pp. 265–91.

Liddington, J. (2006). *Rebel Girls: Their Fight for the Vote*, London, Virago.

Lyon, D. (2000). *Jesus in Disneyland: Religion in Postmodern Times*, Cambridge: Polity Press.

Martin, C. (2014). *Capitalizing Religion: Ideology and the Opiate of the Bourgeoisie*, London: Bloomsbury.

Martin, D. (2005). *On Secularization: Towards a Revised General Theory*, Farnham: Ashgate.

Martin, D. and Catto, R. (2012). 'The religious and the secular', in L. Woodhead and R. Catto (eds), *Religion and Change in Modern Britain*, Abingdon: Routledge, pp. 373–90.

McCall, L. (1992). 'Does gender fit? Bourdieu, feminism, and conceptions of social order', *Theory and Society*, vol. 21, no. 6, pp. 837–67.

Morris, N. and Cant, S. (2006). 'Engaging with place: Artists, site-specificity and the Hebden Bridge Sculpture Trail', *Social and Cultural Geography*, vol. 7, no. 6, pp. 863–88.

Myers, B. (2013). 'Hebden Bridge: A hippie idyll scarred by heroin', *New Statesman (online version)*, 27 November [Online]. Accessed at http://www.newstatesman.com/politics/2013/11/hippie-idyll-scarred-heroin (Accessed 28 January 2019).

Orsi, R. (2005). *Between Heaven and Earth: The Religious Worlds People Make and the Scholars Who Study Them*, Woodstock: Princeton University Press.

Possamaï, A. (2000). 'A profile of New Agers: Social and spiritual aspects', *Journal of Sociology*, vol. 36, no. 3, pp. 364–77.

Possamaï, A. (2002). 'Cultural consumption of history and popular culture in alternative spiritualities', *Journal of Consumer Culture*, vol. 2, no. 2, pp. 197–218.

Primiano, L. (2012). 'Afterword – Manifestations of the religious vernacular: Ambiguity, power and creativity', in M. Bowman and Ü. Valk (eds), *Vernacular Religion in Everyday Life: Expressions of Belief*, Sheffield: Equinox, pp. 231–46.

Prince, R. and Riches, D. (2000). *The New Age in Glastonbury: The Construction of Religious Movements*, Oxford: Berghahn.

Raymond, E. S. (1999). *The Cathedral and the Bazaar: Musings on Linux and Open Source by an Accidental Revolutionary*, Sebastapol, CA: O'Reilly & Associates.

Redden, G. (2005). 'The new age: Towards a market model', *Journal of Contemporary Religion*, vol. 20, no. 2, pp. 231–46.

Rieger, J. and Kwok, P.-l. (2013). *Occupy Religion: Theology of the Multitude*, Lanham, MD: Rowman & Littlefield.

Rowbottom, A. (2012). 'Chronic illness and the negotiation of vernacular religious belief', in M. Bowman and Ü. Valk (eds), *Vernacular Religion in Everyday Life: Expressions of Belief*, Equinox: Sheffield, pp. 93–101.

Sahlins, M. (2011). 'What kinship is (part one)', *Journal of the Royal Anthropological Institute*, vol. 17, no. 1, pp. 2–19.

Stark, R. (1999). 'Secularization, R.I.P', *Sociology of Religion*, vol. 60, no. 3, pp. 249–73.

Stark, R. and Bainbridge, W. S. (1985) *The Future of Religion: Secularization, Revival and Cult Formation*, London: University of California Press.

Sutcliffe, S. (2003). *Children of the New Age*, Abingdon: Routledge.

Sutcliffe, S. (2014). 'New age', in G. Chryssides and B. Zeller (eds), *The Bloomsbury Companion to New Religious Movements*, London: Bloomsbury Academic, pp. 41–5.

Thomas, P. (2008). *Hebden Bridge: A Short History of the Area*, Hebden Bridge: Royd Press.

Tremlett, P.-F. (2013). 'The problem with the jargon of inauthenticity: Towards a materialist repositioning of the analysis of postmodern religion', *Culture and Religion*, vol. 14, no. 4, pp. 463–76.

Tweed, T. (2006). *Crossing and Dwelling: A Theory of Religion*, Cambridge, MA: Harvard University Press.

Voas, D. and Crockett, A. (2005). 'Religion in Britain: Neither believing nor belonging', *Sociology*, vol. 39, no. 1, pp. 11–28.

Vrasidas, C. (2000). 'Constructivism versus objectivism: Implications for interaction, course design, and evaluation in distance education', *International Journal of Educational Telecommunications*, vol. 6, no. 4, pp. 339–62.

Vygotsky, L. (1978). *Mind in Society: The Development of Higher Psychological Processes*, Cambridge, MA: Harvard University Press.

Wanless. C. (2017). 'Individualized religion and the theory of learning', *Journal of the British Association for the Study of Religions (JBASR)*, vol. 18, pp. 11–24.

Warner, R. (2010). *Secularization and Its Discontents*, London: Continuum.

Weber, M. (2009). 'The social psychology of the world religions', in H. Gerth and C. Wright Mills (eds), *From Max Weber: Essays in Sociology*, Abingdon: Routledge, pp. 267–359.

Weber, M. (2012a). *The Protestant Ethic and the Spirit of Capitalism*, Seattle, WA: CreateSpace Independent Publishing Platform / Renaissance Classics.

Weber, M. (2012b). 'The sociology of charismatic authority', in H. Gerth and C. Wright Mills (eds), *From Max Weber: Essays in Sociology*, Abingdon: Routledge, pp. 245–64.

Wenger, E. (1998). *Communities of Practice: Learning, Meaning and Identity*, Cambridge: Cambridge University Press.

Wenger-Trayner, E. and Wenger-Trayner, B. (2015). *Communities of Practice: A Brief Introduction* [online]. Available at: http://wenger-trayner.com/wp-content/upl oads/2015/04/07-Brief-introduction-to-communities-of-practice.pdf (Accessed 28 January 2019).

Willhauck, S. and Thorpe, J. (2001). *The Web of Women's Leadership: Recasting Congregational Ministry*, Nashville: Abingdon Press.

Wilson, B. (1982). 'Secularization and its discontents', in *Religion in Sociological Perspective*, Oxford: Oxford University Press, pp. 148–79.

Wilson, B. (2001). 'Salvation, secularization, and de-moralization', in R. K. Fenn (ed.), *The Blackwell Companion to Sociology of Religion*, Routledge: Blackwell.

Index